U-Boat 202

U-Boat 202

The War Diary of a
German Submarine

by

Lieutenant-Commander
Freiherr Von Spiegel

MEWS BOOKS
LONDON AND CONNECTICUT

Mews Books are published by
Mews Books Limited, 20 Bluewater Hill, Westport, Connecticut 06880
and distributed by
New English Library Limited Barnard's Inn, Holborn, London EC1N 2JR
Made and printed in Great Britain by Hunt Barnard Printing Ltd., Aylesbury, Bucks.

45200032 7

CONTENTS

FOREWORD

This book is a fascinating first-hand account of everyday life aboard a German submarine at sea during the First World War. The translation has been made from the diaries and notes of a successful German naval captain, Lieutenant-Commander Frieherr Von Spiegel, which were originally published in Germany in 1916.

The cruise of duty and the encounters with enemy shipping described by the author is typical of many carried out by German submarines, though this is probably the first time such an intimate view – prejudices and all – has been available. The outward journey of U-Boat 202 is made through the Straits of Dover, and the homeward run, north round the Shetlands.

Although there are undoubtedly some episodes in the book which were specially inserted in the original German for propaganda – *viz.* the minefield episode and the chapter about the alleged misuse of the Red Cross by the English – it was felt that they should not be omitted from this edition so that the whole flavour of Lt-Commander Von Spiegel's narrative should remain just as he wrote it.

These isolated incidents apart, the story of U-Boat 202 still remains a remarkable eye-witness account of the drama and dangers of submarine warfare when it was still very much in its infancy.

THE PUBLISHERS.

CHAPTER I

ON THE WAR-PATH

North Sea	.	.	.	.	12 April 19—.
Course	.	.	.	.	N.W.
Wind	.	.	.	.	S.W., strength, 3 to 4.
State of the Sea	.	.	.	.	3.
Visibility	.	.	.	.	Good.
Both Engines	.	.	.	.	Full speed ahead.

IT was uncomfortable on the conning-tower, as the weather was glorious and the sun shone fiercely on our field-grey leather coats. 'It will soon be summer,' I said to Lieutenant Petersen, who was the officer of the watch and who was sitting next to me on the conning-tower platform; 'I am almost too hot already in my thick underclothing.'

Petersen, who, like myself, was dangling his legs down the hatchway, on the edge of which we were both sitting, put his hand to his neck, as if he also had felt suddenly too hot, and loosened the thick doubly-folded camel's-hair scarf which he was wearing.

'I think I shall soon put this thing out of commission,' he said, and tugged at the faithful friend of the winter, as if he meant to take it off.

'Not yet, my dear fellow; go easy,' said I laughingly. 'Wait until the night comes, and I am sure that you will be only too thankful to put it into commission again.'

'Are we going to run on the surface tonight, Captain, or are we going to submerge?'

'That always depends on the weather,' I replied.

Thus we sat talking and smoking on the conning-tower, whilst our eyes scanned the horizon attentively the whole time, and we kept a sharp look-out all round. The boatswain's mate of the watch stood on the small triangular platform abaft the conning-tower, cleaning the lenses of his binoculars, which had got wet, with a tiny washleather cloth.

'I see that you got wet also, Krappohl,' I called out to him; 'you were not looking out either. That rude fellow made my cigarette wet as well as your glasses. Too bad!'

By 'rude fellow' I meant the spray which had climbed up the conning-tower and reached us quite unexpectedly, in view of the calm weather. Had it been bad weather, I could have borne it. On those occasions we sometimes had not got a dry stitch upon us. Such an impertinent wave, however, coming as a complete surprise in the most perfect weather, is annoying.

We were making good progress. The stem of the boat cleft the water, which rushed past us in two broad white frothy streaks.

The engines rattled and clattered, and the ventilating fan in the control-room, which lay right under our feet, was humming a monotonous song. As the open hatchway was the only outlet for the air, the fan wafted up past our noses all the nice smells from the lower regions. Now there was a smell of lubricating oil, now again, of oranges (we had a large present of them on board), and now – ha, ha, that was coffee, the beautiful, fragrant smell of coffee.

CHAPTER II

THE FIRST SHOT

PETERSEN shuffled restlessly to and fro on the life-belt with which he had upholstered his hard seat, then bent lower into the hatchway, sniffed and said, rubbing his hands contentedly, 'Coffee is almost ready, Captain.'

Just as I had extracted with great difficulty a cigarette case from the breast pocket of my leather coat and was feeling in the remaining pockets for some matches, a hand (size 9½) with outstretched pointing fingers appeared from behind, and the excited voice of the petty officer announced:

'A cloud of smoke in sight four points on the port bow.'

'Quick! the high-power glasses! Where? Ah, yes, there. I see it plainly – '

'Only smoke to be seen, eh?'

Ah, what a strain that was on the nerves. Bent forward, with glasses glued to our eyes, we all three stared at that distant black cloud, which swirled and eddied and was at last blown by the wind into a long thin wisp.

Nothing else was to be seen except the smoke, a sign that the air was clear and transparent as far as the horizon.

What sort of a ship was this which was hidden from our view over the horizon? Was it a harmless cargo steamer, a proud liner, an auxiliary cruiser, or a real heavily armed English cruiser?

These thoughts passed through my brain, resulting in hope and fear – not fear of the enemy, as we were hoping for one, but fear of the disappointment that would be our lot if the ship, when she came nearer, proved to be a neutral steamer.

Seven times in three days we had experienced the same disappointment, seven times had we met neutral ships with no contraband on board, and which we were obliged therefore to allow to proceed on their way. Meanwhile the distance between the ships had been so far decreased that the masts and funnel appeared over the horizon. Two thin slightly raking lines with a thick dark speck between them, therefore – an ordinary cargo steamer. This was what we saw at the first glance. I altered course to north in order to cut off the steamer, which was heading to the eastward. We approached her at full speed, and the bridge and part of the hull soon came into sight.

'Hands to diving stations. Ring the gunnery alarm gong! Gun's crew on deck. First torpedo-tube ready to fire.' I shouted these orders below in a loud voice. Then arose a noise in the voice pipes, such as is caused in a swarm of bees by a stone falling amongst them. The gun's crew sprang from below, climbing the steep ladder close behind one another, clattered through the hatchway, and gained the deck: then they took a deep breath of fresh sea-air to fill their lungs, rolled up their sleeves and fixed their attention upon their gun.

'Can you see any neutral distinction mark, Petersen?'

'No, Captain; the whole side is black. That is an English ship; I can see her flag.'

'Hoist the war ensign! Make the usual signal clearly!' I shouted below into the conning-tower.

Directly afterwards the war ensign fluttered on the flagstaff abaft the conning-tower.

It was saying to them over there: 'Here we are, a German submarine. Now we shall see, proud Briton, who rules the sea.'

We had closed gradually to a distance of six thousand metres. At last an enemy, after so many neutrals – at last a hostile steamer! An ecstatic joy filled us, a joy comparable only with that of the hunter who, after long seeking, sights the quarry at last.

We had travelled many hundreds of miles in storm, wet and cold, and there, two points on the port bow, our first victim beckoned.

Now she must have seen us and recognised our war-flag. Cold fear will have spread through the captain's limbs as he stood on his bridge: The U-boat fear! The U-boat peril! Goddam!

The captain of the cargo steamer did not surrender so easily, however. He sought safety in flight.

Suddenly we saw the steamer belching forth thick black smoke clouds and making a sharp turn away from us to port. The wash under her stern, which had hardly been visible hitherto, now became a frothy mass of white foam, showing that her engines were running at their full power. All to no purpose. However much the captain might storm and swear, and the engineer urge the sweating naked stokers to unheard-of efforts, and however fast the coal might pour on to the glowing furnaces, it would not have helped her. We were gaining, gaining on her with relentless certainty. I had been standing on the top of the conning-tower for some time with my glasses riveted to my eyes, not allowing any movement of the steamer to escape me. Now it appeared to me that the moment had come to issue a peremptory order to stop.

'Fire a shot over the steamer!'

The shell struck the water two hundred metres ahead of her. We waited for a few minutes, and as she did nothing, I gave the gun's crew the correct range and ordered them to fire at her. The second shot hit, and a thick yellow and black cloud of smoke shot up in the air. The third shot tore a piece out of the bulwarks, the fourth hit the bridge, and before the fifth was out out of the muzzle of the gun, the signal was hoisted, 'I have stopped.'

'Ha, ha, old friend, how now!'

An old sea saying runs: 'Caution is the best seamanship.' I

thought it was advisable not to approach any closer for the present, in view of all the tricks and artifices practised against us by the enemy merchant ships. For this reason I stopped my engines too, and hoisted the signal, 'Abandon ship at once!'

As it turned out, the signal was no longer necessary. The English captain had already ordered the abandonment himself when he realised with anger the futility of flight.

A little while afterwards he came alongside in his boat, still angry, handed me the ship's papers in response to my request, and asked me to tow the three boats close to the coast. I promised him to do this, and spoke a few sympathetic words to him on his misfortune and the inexorability of war, which he acknowledged by shrugging his shoulders aggrievedly. After all, I could sympathise with his bad temper.

Then I went and fired a torpedo at the ship, which sank gurgling into the deep with her stern uppermost. Four thousand tons of rice for the English market disappeared with her.

CHAPTER III

A NIGHT JOURNEY

Our first triumph had been achieved and it put us all in a very confident mood. Whatever else might happen, our cruise had not been a fruitless one. As I went down below for a minute and passed along the narrow gangway of the crew space to my own little living-room, I saw beaming faces to right and left of me, and the eyes of each one of them seemed to smile at me as if they wished to say: 'We congratulate you!' The sinking of the steamer was the sole topic of conversation. Those who had seen her go down had to give a description of the event to the remainder, down to the smallest detail: where the torpedo had struck, the height of the column of water, what the steamer had done then, what the people in the boats had looked like, and so on.

As I went back, someone said: 'It will be in the papers tomorrow.' The words stuck in my head for a long time. Yes, tomorrow, in all the German papers, under the heading 'Sunk'; or 'U-Boat's Success', it would be announced that retribution had once more been meted out to our most hated enemy, that the inhuman grip on our people's food supply had again received a strong, severe blow. And away over there on our heartless enemy's island there would be a similar notice in the paper, but this time it would call forth anger and not jubilation.

And some withered-up old Englishman would stare aghast at the telegram in his hand, and scratch his sparse white locks and swear as only an English gentleman can swear.

We towed the three boats belonging to the sunken steamer towards the shore until dusk, and then cast them adrift so as to be free to manoeuvre once more. They were in no further danger, as we were not far from the land and the weather was good. I gave the captain three more bottles of red wine to cheer him up, and sent him off with my best greetings to Mr Churchill and his associates.

The last traces of daylight grew fainter and fainter in the west. The ghost-like red cloud-riders were lengthening out and becoming less defined, and finally drifted apart and disappeared, as if extinguished. In their place came the black demons of the night. They spread over the skies in a pitch-dark mass, hid all the stars and hung loweringly over the sea. It was a night such as we were accustomed to. You could not see your hand in front of your face. The deadlights which covered the little scuttles in the conning-tower were tightly closed so that not even a tiny ray of light could escape. Absolutely invisible we slid through the darkness. Dumb and motionless we sat at our stations – lieutenant, petty officer, and captain – all peering into the darkness and turning our necks ceaselessly from right to left. Our destination was still afar off, and I had to take full advantage of the good weather. I decided, therefore, to remain on the surface all night and to proceed at high speed.[1] Faintly, as from a long way off, a gramophone was singing to us lonely watchers on the conning-tower.

[1] A U-boat travels under water by means of electric motors run off an accumulator battery. The electric power of this battery is used up at a quicker or slower rate according to whether the speed is high or low. In order, therefore, to save the battery-power, the under-water speed is usually very slow. The battery can be re-charged when the boat is running on the surface by means of an oil-driven dynamo. When a high speed is desirable the oil engines are used, and this can only be done when the boat is running on the surface, on account of the large air-supply which is necessary.

'Give me your hand, your dear hand,
Farewell, my love, farewell,
As we journey towards England,
Farewell, my love, farewell,
As we journey towards England.'

What a strange mood possesses me! Here we are in the midst of war, the most violent of all wars! And you are the captain of a submarine, your own submarine, your good, faithful 'U-202', which has carried you bravely and obediently over thousands of of miles and which is going to carry you over many more thousands yet. You are in command of a submarine that has carried death and destruction into the enemy's lines and that dashes through the water like a spirited steed. What are you gazing at in the pitch-black night? Are you thinking of honour and success? Why do your eyes stare so fixedly into the darkness that surrounds you? Perhaps you are thinking of death? Of the innumerable mines floating over there in the darkness? Of the hatred of the enemy who is seeking for you? No, you nerves, you foolish hobgoblins of a foolish mood, I was not thinking of these things. Leave me alone with your idle chatter; I am your captain and you must obey me. Cannot you hear the gentle singing coming up from below, you silly ninnies? Are you too lacking in sense or too faint-hearted to allow it to reach you? Don't you feel the tremendous force of those small thin metallic voices which are wafted up from below? They carry a greeting across twelve hundred miles and through twelve hundred mines.

They extend a small, faithful 'dear' hand towards you, a hand trembling with fear but bravely trusting. Think of them – think of them quietly – but think to yourselves! To outward appearance you must be on the look-out with your powers of vision stretched to their utmost capacity. Your eyes must search all round in the darkness, to right and left, in front and behind.

Binoculars were quickly raised. In the west something had flashed out. A light –

'Hallo, that is somebody.'

'That is no ordinary light, is it?'

Lieutenant Petersen, whom I had addressed, was looking in

an instant through his glasses in the direction of the light.

'I believe that fellow is making a signal,' he said excitedly; 'the light flashes distinctly on and off. I do hope it is not one patrol vessel trying to signal to another.'

Petersen had barely given his verdict on the nature of the unusual light, when we all jumped simultaneously as if we had been electrified, as, suddenly, quite close to us, another series of short signalling flashes was made, which was undoubtedly the answer from what we supposed to be the second patrol vessel, to the first ship's signal.

Great heavens! An enemy ship barely three hundred metres from us! 'Hard a-port! Both engines full speed ahead! Hands to diving stations!' I shouted these orders down into the conning-tower in a lowered voice.

The gramophone in the men's quarters stopped suddenly. Hurried heavy footfalls resounded through the whole boat. The crew were running to their stations. The boat answered her helm promptly and flew round to starboard. The two enemy ships were having a regular conversation.

'Thank God that it is so dark,' said I, breathing freely once more, now that the first danger was over.

'And that the fellow gave away his position by his chatty signals, just as we were about to run into his arms,' was the answer. 'The good God was standing, so to speak, at the wheel.'

The engineer appeared on the ladder leading from the control-room to the conning-tower. 'Permission to go into the engine-room, Captain?'

He was not allowed to leave his diving station in the control-room in the middle of the boat, without asking permission.

'All right, Engineer, you can go and make the engines heave round faster,' I shouted down.

The noise from the heavy oil engines became louder and the note swelled higher and higher, until it became one long-drawn-out loud growl, and the individual knocking sounds which can be heard when going slow disappeared entirely. You could feel that the boat was exerting herself and giving out her utmost capacity.

We were steering a course that would leave the signalling

British ships right astern of us. We went on at high speed for about ten minutes, until the lights had become smaller and less distinct, and then we returned to our original course. We had made a big detour round the enemy ships.

'Like the cat round the hot broth,' said Petersen.

'No, my good fellow,' I said laughingly; 'the comparison is not quite correct, as the cat always comes back, and this broth is too hot for me to do that. But perhaps you are under the impression that I am going to circle round those fellows for hours?'

'Better not, Captain; that might be rather unpleasant for us.'

'Both engines ahead at high speed; hands fall out from diving stations; send the watch on deck.'

The danger was over and the normal night watch could be resumed once more.

We had many more adventures before the morning. The night might have been bewitched. I got hardly any sleep at all. I had only just got below at ten o'clock to my small but snug cabin, where seaman Schuttes, our thoughtful caterer for the whole boat, had spread out on my miniature writing-table the most appetising meal in dishes and tins, accompanied by a bottle of red wine, when the voice-pipe on the bulkhead near my head whistled.

'Whew,' it said loudly, alarmingly, shrilly.

I sprang up, pulled out the whistle-plug and set the mouth-piece to the 'Ready' position.

'A white light two points on the starboard bow.'

I seized cap and gloves and rushed out. Officers' living space, petty officers' space, crew space, each narrower than the last.

'Gangway for the Captain,' shouted the men, and drew their knees out of the way so that I could pass.

'Ach!' I bumped my head hard against the guard round an electric light. As I ran on, I rubbed the injury and swore that the lamp should be removed at the first opportunity. Then through the control-room, up the narrow ladder, and I was on deck.

'Where?'

'There,' pointed Lieutenant Gröning, who was on watch,

'about three points on the starboard bow. It is a steamer. You can see her port bow light plainly. She is crossing our course.'

I put my glasses to my eyes and looked at the light for a few seconds. The officer of the watch's statement was correct. I saw, in addition to the white steaming light, a deep red light, the port bow light. The ship was therefore heading towards our left hand and would cross our course.

A small sickle moon had risen from the sea and was struggling with the darkness of the night. The result was not very promising as the moon was so thin, but even so, the night was not so dark as it had been.

'Don't let her get too close,' I commanded, 'and keep away in plenty of time. We must not be seen, whatever happens, or they will know our destination in England in a very short time; nowadays nearly every steamer has a wireless installation.'

Gröning altered course to starboard until he had the steamer on his port hand.

'It is a pity that we cannot take her with us,' he said.

'No; this is not the right place to make a night attack, you know,' I replied. 'There are too many neutral ships about, and we might easily get a wrong one.'

This happened shortly after ten o'clock. At eleven-twenty, at twelve-forty, at one-ten, at three-fifteen, and at five o'clock, the voice-pipe again whistled 'Whew' alongside my bunk in the captain's quarters. On each occasion I returned from a dream, realised in the fraction of a second that I was wanted on deck, seized cap and gloves, and rushed along the boat, not without bumping my head several times against the frequently cursed electric lamp, to which I have already referred.

CHAPTER IV

A DANGEROUS ENCOUNTER

FROM five o'clock onwards I remained on the bridge, as the dawn, with its uncertain and treacherous light, would soon be breaking, and then the captain's presence on the bridge is imperative, for just as we ourselves were liable to sight another vessel close to us in the dangerous light of the dawning day, so was it just as probable that we should be discovered in our turn; and should the ship in this case prove to be unfriendly, a disagreeable surprise was not unlikely to result. Such a surprise was particularly disagreeable for us, whose strength, as our name implies lies beneath the water, and the smallest splinter of shell can, if it pierces the diving hull and in so doing prevents us from diving again, rob us of our equivalent for Samson's hair.

Shortly before six o'clock I sent the whole crew to diving stations. Everyone stood at his post ready to open or close instantaneously, if ordered, the valve, sluice, or lever which was his particular charge. Only the cook had no station. He stood in his small galley, which was heated electrically, and his only duty was to look after our bodily welfare. He was busy now making coffee, which was the thing most needed at this hour of the day. The whole boat was filled with the fragrant aroma of that coffee, which animated and refreshed our strained nerves and empty stomachs to an extraordinary degree.

Is my meaning clear? I want to ask at this point. Is it quite plain, in the first place, why I give such prominence to the nerves of the U-boat folk and why I refer to them so frequently? Nerves are the all-important feature in submarine officers in time of peace and much more so in time of war. Resolution, strength, endurance, and will-power are all dependent on the condition of our nerves. Nerves are precious possessions, and the most important thing on a voyage is to keep them in good order.

Hour by hour you sit up on top of the conning-tower, whilst underneath you is one of the most intricate mechanisms ever created by human beings, and all around you are the most refined methods for the destruction of that intricate mechanism. Mines, nets, depth-charges, shells, and sharp rams are our enemies. At any moment we may shoot up a hundred metres into the air or sink a hundred metres below the surface of the water. There is danger everywhere; the whole sea is one big powder-magazine. For all this there is only one remedy – Nerves! The whole alphabet of the U-boat science is to come to the right decision at the right instant. One glance must suffice to grasp the situation, and in the same moment, the mind must be made up and the order issued. Every delay is fatal.

I can give you an illustration from something that happened on this very morning.

It was three minutes past six, and the sun would rise in about half an hour's time.

Sea and sky were still merged into one dark-grey colourless mass, and the horizon, which is their junction, could not be seen, and its position could only be guessed. Ceaselessly we scanned the leaden-hued dawn with our glasses. Then suddenly – a shock right through the body – a numb, icy feeling which lasted only for a second. A black shadow appearing in the field of my glasses had made me start. The shadow increased in size, became a ghost of gigantic height and breadth, then took shape, grew more rapidly, became enormous, a black body, a mast, one, two, three, four funnels – a destroyer . . .

'Rapid diving' – 'Ring the alarm' – 'Flood!'

A leap down the hatch into the conning-tower, the water rushed into the diving tanks, the hatchway closed behind me . . . and then the agony of waiting, the counting of seconds, watch in hand, until the tanks are full and the boat dives. Never in my life have such a few seconds seemed to be so long. The destroyer, which had been at most two thousand metres away from us, had naturally sighted us also, and was coming towards us with the full impetus from her forty-thousand-horse-power engines. She was firing at us rapidly from her foremost gun.

'Great God in heaven, if only he fails to hit us!'

A single hit and we are lost.

Already the water reaches the little glass scuttle in the conning-tower, through which I can see the dark ghost chasing us. The bursting of the shells in the sea around us is alarming, they sound like furious hammer strokes on a steel plate, and nearer and nearer come the metallic crashes.

'The rascal is getting our range!'

There – the fifth shot – the whole boat shakes – the next must hit us. Now the treacherous daylight vanishes from the scuttle, the boat answers to the pressure of the diving rudders and submerges.

Red-yellow electric light envelops us, the pointer on the depth indicator climbs up – eight metres, nine metres, ten metres, twelve metres, fourteen metres. Saved!

A sublime, wonderful sensation of safety in the depths of the boundless sea. My heart, which had stopped beating for a few seconds for lack of time, starts once again.

The boat is sinking in truth, deeper and deeper she goes, obeying like a faithful horse the least pressure of the reins, which are represented here by the forward and after hydroplanes or depth-rudders, situated at bow and stern.

Twenty-four metres, twenty-six metres, the depth indicator shows. I had ordered a depth of thirty metres. In the water overhead the crashes and bursts of impotent wrath continue. I turn round and smile at the helmsman, who is standing in the conning-tower with me, a happy smile of safety. I point my thumb upwards. 'Do you hear it, helmsman?'

Silly question, as if he or anyone else in the boat could help hearing it. And yet comprehensible, when you consider the sudden, tremendous tension of the nerves which had to seek release somehow, even in the shape of such a senseless question.

Brave, dear, true boat, how we learn to love you at such times. How we trust in you and would like to embrace you, as if you were a human being, for your intelligence and obedience, and for forgetting all your whims and becoming unselfish when all is dependent on you. We all trust you, all we men on board, just as we also trust each other, united as we are in common danger and in common success:

> 'A common fate awaits us,
> Together we live or die;
> Let true love unite us
> Whilst our lucky star's on high.'

You fair-haired heroes stand down there, ignorant of what is going on over your heads, but feeling nevertheless that every-thing is at stake, that life and death depend on one man's will and one man's resolution. Nevertheless you do your duty with calm assurance, and remain at your stations with mind and body entirely concentrated on your work, trusting with your whole heart in him who is at the same time your leader and your captain. You display the highest form of courage and self-sacrifice, because, though you never see your enemy face to face, yet you manage to fulfil your duty with calmness.

No word was spoken, no voice disturbed the dead silence in the boat. It was possible to forget that all the crew were work-ing down below with nerves a-stretch, translating into life the marvels of the technical appliances around them. The soft hum-ming of the motors was the only sound that could be dis-tinguished and farther and still farther the resounding crash of bursting shells. Suddenly that also ceased. The Englishman had no doubt realised that the fish had given him the slip. Shortly afterwards we heard the angry beat of his propellers in the water. He approached us from our starboard hand with a grinding noise at first soft and distant, but swelling louder and louder like the rustling of the wings of an infinite number of huge birds. He stopped for a short time right over us and then turned back, making the same grinding noise as on his approach, only this time it got fainter as he went away from us.

'Now she has gone away from overhead, did you hear?' I asked the control-room through the voice-pipe.

'Yes, indeed, it was quite plain,' came the brief reply.

I considered what I should do next. Our last move had naturally been to dive as quicky as possible in order to avoid the destroyer which had appeared suddenly in the dawn.

Now, on the contrary, in our submerged condition, we should be fighting with equal chances of success, and I decided to renew the combat with the enemy as soon as the light was good enough to see objects through the periscope. I took advantage of the period of about ten minutes which it was necessary to wait, to send for the long-desired morning coffee, with which to allay the tantalising pangs induced by its fragrant smell, which had been accentuated by the sudden shutting off of the fresh-air supply throughout the boat. Then we crawled cautiously thirty metres upwards from our secure breakfasting position. The higher we got – the depth is read off metre by metre on the depth indicator – the more attentively we listened through the hydrophones for the distant grinding of propellers. The hydrophones, which are affixed to the pressure hull, are the only means of detecting the approach of vessels. In coming to the surface, the critical period lasts from the moment when we reach a depth at which all ships can pass over us safely to the time when the eye can search round through the periscope, because during this period we are blind on account of the opacity of the water and at the same time we are in danger of being rammed and can do nothing to protect ourselves.

No wonder that during this critical period we listened with particular care for the sound of propellers in the vicinity, which alone could warn us of imminent danger whilst we were still unable to see.

Slowly the boat climbed upwards. The top of the periscope

would break surface very soon. Both my hands were clutching the handle by means of which the well-oiled and consequently smoothly-working periscope could be revolved on its axis in a few seconds, and thus give me a rapid all-round survey. My eye was pressed against the indiarubber guard surrounding the eye-piece of the periscope, and was following the rate of ascent of the boat by the increasing clearness and transparency of the water, without having to refer to the depth indicator. More and more the dark inky-hued tint of the deeper water gave way to the bright glass-green colour of the water near the surface, until suddenly white air bubbles were mingled with the water and were followed by a bright silvery light which announced our return to the light of day.

My heart beat with feverish rapidity at the thought of what I might possibly see in my first all-round glance. The destroyer which we had sighted barely a quarter of an hour before might have been a solitary vessel on scouting duty, but she might just as easily have been an advance or flanking ship forming a por-tion of a screen protecting the big battleships. Already my imagination pictured the whole eastern horizon wreathed in the smoke arising from the proud ships under England's flag.

How often during this war has fancy misled us, how often do her flying feet outstrip the dull reality. England's ships – and on a voyage! If you want to read all about that, you must turn over the leaves of a book of fairy-tales. No, England's ships do not venture forth; the fear of the U-boats holds them in check, and keeps them well inside their harbours, chained to their buoys with their heavy anchor-chains.

I saw nothing, absolutely nothing, however carefully I scanned the whole horizon. I did see, however, that it was just beginning to be light, that the glowing red of dawn was spread over the eastern sky, and I saw the last star disappear and the first beam from the rising sun shoot into the sky.

'Dash it all, nothing in sight,' I complained.

'Oh, he'll come back again all right, Captain,' said the helms-man, who was famous for his invincible optimism; 'the broth was too hot for him alone, so he has gone away to fetch a couple of friends.'

'That would not be quite so nice,' interjected my senior lieutenant, Gröning, who was waiting anxiously half-way up the ladder leading from the conning-tower to the control-room; 'no, that would be less agreeable,' he repeated, 'for then the whole mahalla[1] would come with their sweeping wires and depth-charges. That has not been healthy for any of us up to date.'

'You are right there, Gröning,' I had to own; 'it is not pleasant to eat cherries with the English hunting flotillas, when they are armed with so many little devices for our destruction. When they are about, it pays us better to escape, as we have something more valuable to do. It is a pity to waste a good torpedo on such rotten craft.'

However, the little hunting craft did not appear either, so it was no use worrying about them. As we rose still higher and I got an increased height of vision through my periscope, I had another good look round, and saw suddenly to the north-east a curious cloud of black smoke. I did not therefore give the order to come to the surface, but informed the officers in the control-room of the new state of affairs in a few brief words down the voice-pipe, and proceeded at increased speed towards the smoke-cloud.

[1] Mahalla, *i.e.*, swarm of hostile U-boat hunters.

CHAPTER V

THE HORSE TRANSPORT

WE soon made out from the vessel's outline that she was a large steamship going to the westward at high speed. Our first disappointment vanished when we realised beyond a doubt that the fortune of war had again sent an enemy vessel in our direction. We could not see any flag, and there was none hoisted, or we should have been bound to see it. 'Most suspicious,' I thought to myself.

I kept the control-room informed of all my observations through the periscope in the same condensed form as is employed by the vendors of special editions to translate the black headlines of their papers to an expectant public. The word was passed in a whisper from mouth to mouth, until everyone in the boat knew how matters stood on deck. Each fresh bit of information that was sent down from the conning-tower increased the tension of the highly expectant crew, and I do believe that if there were such an instrument as a barometer for measuring the tension of human nerves, then would the pointer surely have reached its highest mark as the words fell like hammer blows into the control-room:

'The steamer is armed!'

'Have a peep, helmsman,' I said, as I moved away from the periscope. 'Can you see the gun in front of the bridge?'

'Yes, indeed,' came the quick and excited reply, 'I can see it; rather a big one.'

'And now look aft, just abaft the second mast – what do you see there?'

'Great Scot! Another gun – a four-inch at the very least. That is a transport.'

'Lower the periscope! Port ten degrees,' I ordered.

'Torpedo-tube ready,' the torpedo-mate reported through the voice-pipe from the forward torpedo-room.

I had the periscope lowered far enough to ensure that its top was completely submerged, so that from now onwards those on board the steamer would see nothing of us, even with the most careful look-out.

'Advance to the attack,' was the watchword.

Oh, that delightful sensation of the power of the U-boat's grip! The splendid co-operation of the boat and her crew, of inert machinery and energetic men! The blending together in a single harmonious body of the steel and nerves and spirit of a thousand inanimate things with the whole human element.

'Yes, the ship is like a live creature,' the thought passed through my mind, as I proceeded towards the enemy with the periscope housed, 'like a large creeping cat, with back arched and bristling whiskers. The eye is represented by the periscope, the brain by the conning-tower, the heart by the control-room, the legs by the machinery, and the teeth and claws by the torpedoes.'

Silently we crept closer and closer, in a state of great excitement. It was most important that our periscope should not be seen, so that the steamer could not turn away and make good her escape at the last minute. I raised the extreme tip of the periscope above water with great care every few minutes, took a brief look at the steamer, and lowered it down again quickly. This was sufficient to enable me to see as much as I wanted to.

The steamer was crossing our course rapidly from starboard to port. I estimated her speed at sixteen knots, by the height of the foaming mass of water driven up around her bows. The hunter realises how necessary it is for him to know the speed of his quarry when he is shooting. He does not aim as far ahead at a wounded hare as he does at one which is in full flight. I had only to guess the speed, for which purpose a seaman has a good eye, and then to ascertain by the help of a Table the exact angle for which I must make allowance.

Having found the angle, I set it on to a graduated disc which was fitted on the periscope, and then, if I fired the torpedo at the same moment in which the steamer came opposite the zero mark of the periscope, the torpedo would hit.

You see, the thing is quite simple. I manoeuvre the boat into position, aim through the periscope and fire when the right moment has come. Anyone who wants to know all the details of how it is done, must join the navy, or, if he is too old to do so himself, he must send us his son or his nephew.

On this occasion everything went splendidly. The steamer could not see our periscope, which was exposed cautiously at rare intervals, and she continued stupidly to steer her old course. The depth-keeping arrangements in the control-room were working beautifully and made my task of creeping close unseen much easier.

Already I could distinguish the details of things on deck. The steamer appeared to be close to us and looked colossal. I saw the captain walking on his bridge, a small whistle in his mouth. I saw the crew cleaning the deck forward, and I saw, with surprise and a slight shudder, long rows of wooden partitions right along all the decks, from which gleamed the shining black and brown backs of horses.

'Oh, heavens, horses! What a pity, those lovely beasts!'

'But it cannot be helped,' I went on thinking. 'War is war, and every horse the fewer on the Western front is a reduction of England's fighting power.' I must acknowledge, however, that the thought of what must come was a most unpleasant one, and I will describe what happened as briefly as possible.

There were only a few more degrees to go before the steamer would be on the correct bearing. She would be there almost

immediately; she was passing us at the proper distance, only a
few hundred metres away.

'Stand by for firing a torpedo!' I called down to the control-
room.

That was a cautionary order to all hands on board. Everyone
held his breath.

Now the bows of the steamer cut across the zero-line of my
periscope – now the forecastle – the bridge – the foremast –
funnel –

'Fire!'

A slight tremor went through the boat – the torpedo had
gone.

'Beware, when it is released!'

The death-bringing shot was a true one, and the torpedo ran
towards the doomed ship at high speed. I could follow its course
exactly by the light streak of bubbles which was left in its wake.

'Twenty seconds,' counted the helmsman, who, watch in
hand, had to measure the exact interval of time between the
departure of the torpedo and its arrival at its destination.

'Twenty-three seconds.' Soon, soon this violent, terrifying
thing would happen. I saw that the bubble-track of the torpedo
had been discovered on the bridge of the steamer, as frightened
arms pointed towards the water and the captain put his hands
in front of his eyes and waited resignedly. Then a frightful
explosion followed, and we were all thrown against one another
by the concussion, and then, like Vulcan, huge and majestic, a
column of water two hundred metres high and fifty metres
broad, terrible in its beauty and power, shot up to the heavens.

'Hit abaft the second funnel,' I shouted down to the control-
room.

Then they fairly let themselves go down below. There was a
real wave of enthusiasm, arising from hearts freed from sus-
pense, a wave which rushed through the whole boat and whose
joyous echoes reached me in the conning-tower. And over
there? War is a hard task-master! A terrible drama was being
enacted on board the ship, which was hard hit and in a sinking
condition. She had a heavy and rapidly increasing list towards
us.

All her decks lay visible to me. From all the hatchways a storming, despairing mass of men were fighting their way on deck – grimy stokers, officers, soldiers, grooms, cooks. They all rushed, ran, screamed for boats, tore and thrust one another from the ladders leading down to them, fought for the life-belts and jostled one another on the sloping deck. All amongst them, rearing, slipping horses were wedged. The starboard boats could not be lowered on account of the list; everyone therefore ran across to the port boats, which, in the hurry and panic, had been lowered with great stupidity either half-full or over-crowded. The men left behind were wringing their hands in despair and running to and fro along the decks; finally they threw themselves into the water so as to swim to the boats.

Then – a second explosion, followed by the escape of white hissing steam from all hatchways and scuttles. A boiler must have burst. The white steam drove the horses mad. I saw a beautiful long-tailed dapple-grey horse take a mighty leap over the berthing rails and land into a fully-laden boat. At that point I could not bear the sight any longer, and I lowered the periscope and dived deep.

When I came up again some time afterwards there was nothing left to be seen of all that proud ship. Three boats were floating amongst the debris and the dead bodies of horses, and were picking up stray swimmers. Now I came to the surface, to lend them a hand. When they saw the vast whale-like form of our hull rise suddenly in their midst they were seized with panic, and tugged feverishly at their oars in an effort to escape. Only when I climbed out on top of the conning-tower and waved my handkerchief and cap did they stop pulling and finally came nearer.

Some of them were in pitiable plight, having nothing on but thin linen trousers and a handkerchief wrapped round the neck. The iron ration which every boat is obliged to carry was not sufficient for them, as the crews were double or treble their proper numbers.

CHAPTER VI

SURROUNDED

WHILST I was still discussing with our victualling petty officer what we could spare under these circumstances from our own stores, many clouds of smoke, rapidly drawing nearer, were sighted in the north and west. It dawned upon me at once: 'They are looking for you now; here comes the whole "mahalla"!' Already the typical masts of English destroyers and trawlers[1] could be distinguished, so that we had not a moment to lose to escape from these the most dangerous of all enemies.

Having quickly made up my mind, I called out to the captain of the sunken ship that one of the vessels which were approaching from the northward would pick him up, that I had no time to do so myself and must be getting away to the north-eastward. Thereupon I dived in sight of the shipwrecked crew and shaped a north-easterly course, which I maintained for some little time and then lowered the periscope and altered my course to

---

[1] Armed English trawlers, fitted with sweeping lines for locating us, and with depth-charges, which explode under water, for dropping upon us when found.

south without being seen.

After a little while, I took another look round cautiously, and was astonished to see that a long line of hunting vessels was closing upon us from the southward as well. From three sides the enemy bloodhounds were hot upon our tracks, and I made out that it would not be very long before the ring was complete and the western side blocked as well, by the closing in of the various groups, and then the hunt for the big tin fish would begin.

I must own that I was not feeling very happy, as, to start with, the depth of the sea in the whole neighbourhood was not sufficient to enable us to escape from the combined operations of the nets, sweeps, and depth-charges.

'The wild cat has become a hare,' passed through my mind, and I had now to decide once and for all what course to pursue.

Since we have become a hare, we must copy the example of Mümmelmann's old man hare near Löns – that is to say, we must first hop carefully forward with eyes open, taking every advantage of cover, find the place where the guns were standing farthest apart, and then escape from our difficulty by springing through the broadest gap with eyes closed.

Our next move was, therefore, to shape an easterly course, as this was the only direction in which things, as yet, were not too warm for us.

Now and again I flashed the periscope up to the surface and observed the gradual drawing-in of the circle. Now that my mind was made up, I had become quite calm and was examining the pros and cons freely and carefully.

Just as in the real hare-drive, the whole collection of vessels began to close in towards the centre as soon as the circle was complete. Between every pair of beaters – I should have said trawlers – which had a sweep passed between them, was a small squat torpedo-boat – corresponding to the gunner – which was towing explosive charges astern.

In the north, a gap had been caused by the closing-in of the wing towards the east. Further, I saw that one of the torpedo-boats belonging to the northern group, which was stationed between two of the groups of sweeping trawlers, had steamed away towards the boats of the wrecked ship. In that direction lay our best chance of escape. I steered towards the gap between the two pairs of trawlers. Of course, our periscope remained practically invisible the whole time.

The line of tracking hounds came slowly nearer, smoking and snorting. Now the time had come to follow the second half of old Mümmelmann's programme. Therefore I closed my eyes – in other words, I lowered the periscope completely and descended at increased speed to the greatest possible depth.

I can well imagine what was demanded of old man hare in that blind run for his life. We certainly shared many mutual sensations. The small gap towards which we were heading could be so easily filled up by a slight lateral movement of the sweeping craft. And should we, then, be entangled in one of the network sweeps, there would be little hope of escape. The enemy would rush towards us from all sides, and, by means of bombs and depth-charges, would send us to utter destruction on the bottom of the sea.

No one in the boat dreamt of the danger through which we were passing. I had kept all my observations on the encircling tactics of the enemy to myself, and had given nothing away, so as not to excite the crew unnecessarily. After all, no one could alter the situation.

Now the information came from the foremost, or bow, compartment: 'Sounds of propellers on the port side!' I heard these sounds myself shortly afterwards in the conning-tower, a soft, slowly swelling, grinding sound; that was not the sound from a rapidly revolving destroyer's propeller, which produces a much higher and louder note; that was the dull slow beat from the propellers of the heavy sweeping trawlers.

I leaned over to the starboard side anxiously. . . . Nothing to be heard. That was a good sign, for then I could hope that we had hit off the gap and that the propeller sound which we heard to port proceeded from the inner trawler on the left side of the gap. Just as my heart wanted to shout hurrah, a fresh noise was heard, exactly ahead. High, sharp, grinding, it rang louder and nearer. That was the torpedo-boat; oh dear – the beast! Why must the infernal rascal be resuming his station again just at the right moment?

The torpedo-boat only took a few seconds to pass over us. They seemed to be like hours. Each moment I thought I heard something bumping, piercing, and crashing into us, and imagined my beautiful boat cracked like an empty eggshell. But fortune was on our side. The sharp grinding noise from the torpedo-boat's whizzing propeller grew fainter and fainter and finally died away altogether. I drew myself up a little, unconsciously, in the conning-tower and whistled a few bars from 'Puppchen' and tapped the glass of the depth-indicating instrument with the knuckle of my first finger, as if nothing had happened. What do you say? Nothing had happened; everything was in perfect order. The depth was correct, the depth-rudders lay in their normal position; there in front of me stood Tuzcynski, my faithful depth-keeper, and servant, formerly a fisherman in the waters of the Vistula and Nogat; and behind me the helmsman leant comfortably against the wall of the conning-tower and yawned.

I had, suddenly, a tremendous longing for a cigarette; my nerves required a stimulant. I waited another ten minutes, and then let the boat ascend to periscope depth and had a look at the scene of the hunt. What I saw filled my heart with joy. The whole mob had drawn away to the south-westward, and was continuing the search in a long line in that direction. As we were going on opposite courses, the distance between us was rapidly increasing. In another five minutes I could take the risk of coming to the surface. All was clear to the northward.

I was soon sitting on the top of the conning-tower in a happy frame of mind, and was drawing the precious sea-air greedily into my lungs, whilst I puffed away at my good cigarette at the same time.

CHAPTER VII

A RICH PRIZE

In the late afternoon of the same day we came upon a harmless fishing flotilla, like a wolf upon a sheep-fold. In order to be certain that there was no shepherd, with his dog, keeping watch, we had made, whilst still submerged, as close an inspection of each vessel as possible.

I could not discover anywhere a gun or anything else suspicious; they were all lying peacefully engaged upon their nets, which were several kilometres long. There were seven steam drifters and nine sailing drifters scattered over an area of about three miles square.

The weather was even finer than it had been the day before. The sun was laughing down from the steel-blue sky, and dancing in golden beams on the glassy sea. A very light breeze from the northward caused the fishing boats to roll to and fro slightly, so that the gaffs and booms, on which the spare nets were hanging, lazily swung and banged. Enormous masses of snow-white seagulls were flying about in the neighbourhood of the flotilla, clustering in inquisitive, squawking masses over the

stern of each individual boat, and plunging in steep dives on to
the offal from the last catch, which the fishermen threw over-
board. The line of the horizon separating sea and sky was as
sharp as a knife, and encircled us like a large luminous disc. No
clouds of smoke tarnished its clear outline. There was nothing
in sight except our friends the fishermen.

Ah, this was the kind of weather for us! It was a favourable
opportunity, rarely offered, of striking a blow at England's fish
market. I rose suddenly, like a ghost, close astern of one of the
steam drifters, threw open the conning-tower hatch, and sprang
out on top of the tower, holding in one hand the fluttering war
ensign, and in the other, the megaphone.

'Halloooooo!'

The fishermen opened their mouths and stared at us dully, as
if paralysed with terror.

'Hallooo, Capt'n!' I shouted in English for the second time. 'I
want to talk with you!'

After a pause, one figure detached itself from the motionless
crowd, climbed up the ladder to the bridge, got hold of a
speaking-trumpet and shouted a few inarticulate words through
it, which must have meant something like 'Here I am'.

I mustered my best English and informed the red-nosed individual that all the fishing boats round about would be sunk
before sunset. I told him, further, that I had detailed him to
collect all the other crews on board his drifter, and that he must
cut his net adrift at once without any further argument, and
follow me at a distance of five hundred metres; that he would
be immediately blown into the air if he did not maintain this
distance exactly, and if he did not do so, I should suspect him of
the hostile intention of ramming me.

The captain said that he understood everything clearly, cut
away his net, and followed astern of me.

I ran the engines at high speed, hoisted the signal 'Abandon
ship immediately' at my masthead, and darted amongst the
frightened flock. The sailors stood at their guns with sparkling
eyes, holding the shells affectionately in their arms, waiting
until I let them make a start. We steered a zig-zag course right
through the flock once, and then went round the circum-

ference, in order to prevent the more distant ones from making an attempt at escape. We did not stop to sink any of the ships whose crews were being taken off, as they could no longer get away from us. How quickly the men in the ships close at hand got out! They clambered hurriedly into their boats from fear of our shells. The water was soon covered with dinghies and cutters, and the salvage drifter was laden with men.

In spite of the exciting occupation, we did not forget to keep a sharp look-out so that there should be no chance of our being surprised at our work. Nothing appeared in the distance, however, and the horizon remained clear and empty.

When all the fishermen were assembled on board the one drifter, we started sinking the remainder. We went from ship to ship, stopping a hundred metres away and firing slow, well-aimed shots at their waterlines, until they had had enough and sank. Some sank after the first shot, but others were tougher and needed four shots. It was fine sport for the guns' crews. The men stood in a row and took turns at firing, eagerly counting the shots that each one needed for his 'fish'. When we had finished with all the steam drifters, we went on to the sailing drifters, which lay in a group all together, according to their custom and an old-established habit of co-operation. They mostly needed only one shot, and then heeled over and sank gurgling into the deep. It was a moving sight, which got on our nerves each time, in spite of our secret joy, because every real seaman sees in the sailing ship the last scanty trace of the romance of sea-life, which is fast dying out. That is the reason, at all events, why we felt sad on this and on later occasions, whenever we sank a sailing ship.

The surface of the water over a large area was covered with hundreds of thousands of dead fish, which formed a most welcome dish for a vast number of gulls, which did themselves well on the tempting fare, and went on eating and stuffing themselves until the feathers stuck out on their stomachs.

We had already sunk thirteen drifters. Two sailing drifters and the steam drifter with the crews on board were all that remained of the whole flotilla. As it was an opportunity which seldom occurred, I had allowed the stokers and engine-room artificers to come on deck in turns, so that they might see the sinking of a ship with their own eyes for once. I enjoyed listening to their comical remarks and watching the childish glee with which every fresh shot was welcomed. It pleased me to see the bright colour which fresh air and excitement produced in their pale faces.

Gröning came across to me and said in a thoughtful tone: 'What will happen when the steam drifter gets back and gives away our position? The English could trace our course exactly after the events which took place yesterday afternoon, early this morning, and now?'

'Dash it all, you are right there! I had never even thought of that. I must be getting old and feeble-minded. Whatever happens we must prevent that, more especially as tomorrow – well, you understand, don't you?'

Gröning nodded.

'Yes, tomorrow will be a heavy day,' I went on to say; 'we must not make it more difficult for ourselves than necessary, or we shall not get through it.'

I thought quickly how to remove the risk of being reported by the fishermen, without endangering their lives, which I would not do under any circumstances. Suddenly I gave myself a smack on the forehead and laughed.

'Too stupid – one never thinks of the most simple things! I tell you what, Gröning; we will simply transfer the whole party to one of those two sailing ships. It will take them at least three days to reach the coast in this light wind, and then it won't matter to us. It will be a bit crowded for all those people, but that cannot be helped.'

'What about provisions?' Gröning interposed. 'How are they going to exist?'

'Oh, that won't be very difficult,' I replied. 'In the first place, they can take the food over from the steam drifter with them, and they will have, in addition, all the fish which are lying in the hold of the sailing vessel.'

Having settled what to do, I had the smaller of the two remaining sailing drifters sunk, and then went over to the steam drifter which had the shipwrecked crews on board.

The captain was naturally bitterly disappointed when I broke the bad news to him that they were all to shift over. He had been so delighted at being the one selected to retain his ship. On the other hand, the captain of the sailing drifter rejoiced exceedingly when he heard the news that he was to return to his faithful old ship, and regarded the tidings as a special inter-position of Providence. Truly joy and sorrow go hand-in-hand.

A short half-hour later the trans-shipment was complete, and the steam drifter sank into the deep – the fifteenth ship in two hours. The sailing drifter commenced by hauling in her net carefully, and then crawled away to the westward with flapping sails.

CHAPTER VIII

A NIGHT ON THE
BOTTOM OF THE SEA

THAT night we lay on the bottom of the sea near X——. We wanted to get a good night's rest once more, in order both to make up for our lost sleep and to accumulate a reserve for the days which were to follow. It is very comfortable lying on the soft sandy bottom of the North Sea. It is exactly as if the whole ship was put to bed. But it needs to be calm on the surface, as otherwise the motion is felt even at great depths, and the boat is thrown about all over the place. Then it is Hell!

Slowly the boat glided deeper and deeper. We had previously taken an approximate sounding with the hand lead. I let the motors run slower as we approached the bottom of the sea, and finally I stopped them altogether when we could only have been a few metres off the bottom. As soon as the boat had lost her headway, which we knew by the fact of the hydroplanes ceasing to have any effect on her, a few hundred litres of water were admitted into a ballast tank specially constructed for the purpose, which caused the boat to become heavier and to descend gently.

'She is just going to bump,' I shouted down into the control-room, with my eye on the depth indicator.

The words were barely out of my mouth when there was quite a gentle shock – very much more gentle than when a train stops – and we were lying on the bottom. We quickly admitted some more water into the ballast tanks so as to make the boat rest more heavily on her bed, and then everyone searched his allotted portion of the hull carefully to see that no water was coming in through valves or scuttles.

The report came from forward and aft, 'All tight!' I let the crew fall out after the necessary watches and rounds had been arranged. 'All hands to rest!' was the order of the day.

An evening's rest on the bottom! No other evening's rest can be compared with it. An evening's rest after so much excitement and such a day's work. Can anyone realise how much we enjoyed it? We did not worry about the fact that we were not in harbour and that a mountain of water lay overhead; we felt as safe and snug as if we had been in the most secure place in the world.

The crew passed by us on their way forward from the eight spaces, the stern compartment, and the engine-room. Pale faces, smeared with oil and dirt, but with eyes beaming at me with pride and happiness as they went by, in a manner that rejoiced my heart.

Gaiety reigned in the crew spaces. They splashed and washed themselves, all talking and laughing together, so that you could see how happy and free from care they felt.

'Now, what are we going to have to eat today?' I asked the cook, who was standing, engrossed and self-conscious – for he was an artist in his own line – before his small stove, stirring the contents of a steaming nickel saucepan. 'That smells wonderfully appetising!'

'Beef stew with salt potatoes,' the cook replied, and fell to stirring his saucepan with redoubled vigour. 'It is just ready,' he continued, 'it will not be more than five minutes.'

'Oh dear, in that case I must hurry up.'

So saying, I went forward to my cabin, which I had not entered since five o'clock that morning. I hung up my cap, scarf, and leather jacket on a hook, stretched myself in weary content in my sweater, and allowed myself to enjoy thoroughly a good wash of face and hands with soap and hot water, a rare luxury on a long journey. From next door the lively movements and conversation of the officers were wafted over to me.

Then plates rattled, a cork popped, and Gröning opened the small door that separated my cabin from the officers' mess: 'Dinner is ready, Captain.'

We were soon sitting, a party of four, round the clean nicely-laid little table, attacking the contents of the steaming dishes with lusty appetite, and drinking precious sparkling Canary wine out of small cups. The events of the past day had to be toasted with a little of the best wine we had on board. We had always made a practice of doing this when the fortune of war favoured us.

The electric radiators gave out a gentle heat, which had this disadvantage, however, that the heat rose in the absolutely still atmosphere, with the result that the floor was several degrees colder than it was just under the deck overhead. But all the same we felt very comfortable in our thick sea-boots. The gramophone played without ceasing. The petty officers had taken charge of it, and were playing one patriotic song after another upon it. How they inspired us! All was suddenly still in the boat. German patriotic songs sung on the deep-sea bottom, close to England's shores! German hearts were fired with enthusiasm and uplifted by the notes of the music to make a silent pledge to give of their best to the Fatherland, to be a terror to the enemy, and to damage him in every possible way.

Some such thoughts were doubtless in most of our minds, perhaps less poetically expressed, but none the less of good intention. After this, dances, operettas, and rag-time music were played, and induced a less solemn but thoroughly happy mood. The stokers and seamen were having a particularly cheery time. Merry songs were heard coming from their quarters, and dirty old playing cards were produced and a lively game of real German Skat indulged in. Meanwhile, in the officers' quarters, we were raising our glasses and clinking them to the U-boats' own toast: 'Good hunting and a safe return.

Good luck to the U-boats!'

The boat was lying wonderfully steady. She did not move an inch.

'Here is an original idea for a painter,' said the engineer, who was poetically inclined, as he leaned back in his chair and gazed thoughtfully at the deck overhead. 'Picture to yourself a cross-section of the boat through our mess-room: outside, the yellow sand dunes of the North Sea bottom, alive with all sorts of creeping, swimming denizens of the sea; inside, four laughing officers seated at dinner round a small table illuminated by the warm electric light, the bottle of Canary wine in the centre, the glasses raised on high for the solemn toast. Overhead, as high as a church-tower, water – water – water – and above that again the glistening starry vault of heaven and a small silver moon. Were I a painter, I would start on that subject at once.'

'And I hope you would present the picture to me,' I laughed. 'It is really not at all a bad idea; someone ought to suggest it seriously to a painter.'

'Perhaps you would also permit a couple of mermaids to come into the picture; they would be looking curiously through the scuttles of the conning-tower and tapping with their fingers on the glass,' came from Petersen, our youngest member, accompanied by sly laughter; 'that would make the picture more attractive.'

Gröning, who had been sitting listening to all our conversation in smiling silence, slowly removed from his mouth his empty amber cigarette-holder, which he was always chewing when under water, because, as a heavy smoker, he suffered from being unable to smoke, and said, with light irony in his deep sympathetic voice: 'Man, Petersen, you are really an incorrigible youth. When there is no woman in the plot, it is incomplete for you from the start. There you are, thinking again of mermaids, and you declare every month that you want to become engaged. "It really is quite certain this time", "This time I am certainly going to do it", "I shan't get another one like this one", and so on. Every month I have to listen to that. What was the name of the last one you wanted to make happy, the March lady? Hold on; I have forgotten. The February bride

– ha, ha, ha – does the Captain know the story of the February bride?' he turned to me, laughing.

'Will you be quiet, Gröning?' interrupted Petersen, blushing to the tips of his ears. 'I promise you, that if you talk out of school; besides – '

'Come on, Petersen,' I encouraged him, as he suddenly stopped, 'besides what?'

'Besides, there is no truth in any of it,' he rattled cheerfully on, becoming even redder as he saw that he had given himself away. 'You had better be quite quiet,' he went on, beaming suddenly, as he passed to the attack in order to get the conversation away from himself. 'Whoever lives in a glass palace, as you do, should be a little more careful.'

'I? What do you mean? That is really the limit!' retorted Gröning, who was very fond of posing to his comrades as a complete woman-hater. 'I in a glass palace? That is a mean accusation; but perhaps you have partaken too freely of the juice of the berry, youngster – what?'

'Rubbish! only one glass,' replied the youth. 'It is ridiculous to make such a statement.'

'Now, gentlemen, don't quarrel,' I interposed soothingly; 'what you need is a good rest. We do not want to quarrel here on the bottom of the sea. I make the decision herewith, that our youngster is quite sober, but that nevertheless he may not introduce his April bride with the fish-tail as a punishment for having disowned his February bride; for to have withheld a good story from us tonight – and I take it from you that it was a good story, young fellow – is a crime well deserving of punishment.'

Our two happy fighting cocks, who were incidentally the best friends in the world, had to be content with my finding, and the everlasting problem of Eve and her daughters, which even here at the bottom the the sea had nearly produced a quarrel, was shelved.

Shortly afterwards we lay down in our small beds to rest, taking off our clothes for the first time since the beginning of our voyage, and seeking refuge in a dreamless and beneficial slumber.

CHAPTER IX

THROUGH THE MINEFIELD

No cock crowed to wake me in the morning. Whence could he have crowed? However, in his place, my faithful servant, Tuczynski the Pole, stood beside my bed and announced: 'Five-thirty, Captain!'

I sat up, drowsy and bewildered after my deep sleep. 'What is the matter?'

'Five-thirty,' repeated the servant; 'everything is all ready for you to wash and dress.'

Ach, yes! I returned to my senses suddenly. We were lying on the bottom. In an hour's time we should rise to the surface, and then – With one bound I was out of bed. The thought of the 'then' had quickly made me wide awake. 'Then it would happen, today it would happen,' I went on thinking as I put on my slippers.

Barely was I on my feet, when I had to support myself by placing my hand upon the wardrobe, so as not to lose my balance.

'Hallo,' I turned in astonishment to the honest Pole, who was just spitting upon my left sea-boot to make it shine, 'so we are rolling. What is the matter?'

'There must be a bit of a sea running up topsides,' he replied, grinning.

'I could have thought that out for myself, fathead; but when did it begin? Run along and ask at what time we commenced to roll.'

Tuczynski hurried off to the control-room and came back immediately with the information: 'Since about two o'clock this morning, Lieutenant Petersen says.'

'There must be a fair amount of sea running, if we have been rolling for four hours. You might put out my oilskin, as it will be wet today,' I ordered, and went on dressing myself hurriedly and in the best way possible to keep out the wet.

The change of weather which had undoubtedly occurred during the night did not suit my plans at all well. As far as I could judge from the motion of the boat, the weather was not as yet very bad, perhaps a wind of strength six.

In all probability it would soon get bad. It had become considerably worse, and could get very nasty at this time of year.

'Damn it all, on this day of all days!' I cursed into my six days' stubble.

After breakfast I collected the whole crew in the control-room.

'Men,' I addressed them, 'you know that we have still got hard work in front of us. We are only at the beginning of our undertaking. We had good luck yesterday and the day before; we have just had a peaceful night. We are all going fully rested and in happy confidence to our new day's work. We are going to pass today through the so-called Witches' Cauldron. You all know what I mean, and you know also that it is no light undertaking. The enemy keeps a deuced sharp look-out there. Good! – we will keep a better. Others have got through before us, so we shall get through also, if everyone remains at his post and does his duty as well as he has done up to date. That I expect from every man on board. To your diving stations!'

I went into the conning-tower. The engineer announced

shortly afterwards from the control-room: 'All hands are at their diving stations!'

Now we could make a start. The day began. It was to be the most remarkable day in my life.

'Let her come to the surface!'

The pump began to rattle. This was what had to be done. The water, which had been admitted into the ballast tanks to give the boat negative buoyancy – that is to say, a tendency to fall – had to be pumped out until the boat had a little positive buoyancy, and began to rise of her own accord. This manoeuvre had been usually very successful. Today, on the contrary, the boat hung; she 'stuck', as we generally call it.

Involuntarily I thought of the question which is asked repeatedly by civilians: 'Are you not afraid that you will never come up again?' Naturally we were not afraid, but from sheer habit my fingers tapped impatiently on the glass front of the depth indicator, to see if the pointer would not move at last.

'Nine hundred litres more than usual,' Engineer Krüger announced from below.

That meant that we had pumped nine hundred more litres of water out of the boat than was usually necessary to make her lift.

'We are properly stuck in the chalk,' I said jestingly. 'According to the chart, there should certainly be a sandy bottom here.'

'Now she is getting free!' shouted the engineer.

Yes indeed, she rose – the pointer of the depth indicator climbed upwards – but she came up at an angle, with her stern uppermost and her snout stuck in the mud.

'What a dirty trick,' I heard Gröning, who was in charge of the depth-rudders, swearing; 'now her whole trim will be upset.'

That was a fact, as we had now to trim her down aft, and go through the weary procedure of upsetting the correct trim by pumping water from the forward tanks into the after tanks, in order to make the boat lighter forward and heavier aft. After a few hundred litres had been shifted in this manner, the boat bethought herself of her duty towards us and assumed once more the horizontal position. Now she rose bravely and steadily, but showed a tendency to trim in the opposite direction – that is to say, down by the stern, as was only to be expected until we trimmed her back to the proper distribution of weights.

After the boat had apparently done her best to resist our efforts to get her away from her sand-bed on the bottom, she naturally could not stick her nose up into the fresh air quickly enough to please herself. With nine hundred litres of positive buoyancy she shot upwards. But I was of another opinion, as I thought it would be wise to put up a feeler in the shape of the periscope first, in order to see that the air was free from germs. As I felt myself entirely responsible for the health of my boat, I entertained an apprehension, grounded on experience, that the bacilli represented by waiting destroyers or trawlers could be unhealthy, and I therefore opposed her wishes strenuously, and by readmitting the nine hundred litres of water into her again, subdued the rapid climb.

I started the motors at the same time so as to get headway on and enable the depth-rudders to be worked, and I ordered a depth of twenty metres to be maintained.

Then I went quickly to periscope depth and searched the surface of the water for any sign of ships. Nothing was in sight, but – oh dear – quite a heavy sea was running.

'Well, it can't be helped,' I said to myself softly, took another look round the horizon, and came right out on to the surface. Ha, that was a pleasure, when I stood on top of the conning-tower shortly afterwards, and, with my hands pressed to my sides, filled my lungs with fresh sea-air. The air in the boat had really not been bad – on the contrary, the engineer had kept it unusually fresh last night – but still the fresh sea-air was nicer.

The ventilating fan was already purring as it brought relief right throughout the boat to those who had to remain down below.

'Now, helmsman, you can bring me the chart again. Yes, all right, you can put it here on top of the conning-tower; it won't matter if it does get wet. Now the compasses and pencil! Good, thank you.'

'Now, pay attention and check my calculations, to see that I don't make a mistake. It is exactly twenty-two miles from here to the first minefield. From there to the second minefield is fourteen miles, making a total of thirty-six miles. We must time ourselves to reach the first minefield shortly before low water, on the last of the ebb-tide, as the mines are only visible from a little before to a little after low water. It is six-thirty now, and low water is at ten o'clock. We can therefore proceed comfortably at half-speed and have plenty of time to recharge the batteries. Is that right?'

'Quite right,' replied the helmsman, hastily folding up the chart, which he had been anxiously sheltering with his body, the whole time it lay on top of the conning-tower, from the spray which came over us from time to time, 'if only we have not got to dive again in the meanwhile.'

'I don't think we shall have to,' I answered confidently. 'Surely there will be no other vessels in the neighbourhood of the minefield; we ought to be safer here than anywhere else. We must begin to look out when we get to the other side.'

Punctually at one hour before low water we reached the neighbourhood in which the enemy believed that he had blocked the channel to hostile U-boats, by means of an extensive minefield laid in several lines. I say 'believed', because the mines, as already mentioned, float on the surface of the water round about the time of low water, and then we simply slip through the gaps, so that the blocking of this important channel was perhaps a comforting, but rather costly illusion on the part of the enemy. I did not find it quite so simple a matter to slip through the mines as the reports of my brother officers had led me to believe.

'So, gentlemen, now the fun begins!' I said to the two officers, who had crept close to me in their thick oilskins, having exchanged their uniform caps decorated with the oak-leaves for the practical sou'-wester. 'Now we will see who sights the first mine.'

We stood close to one another in a shower of foam and spray and gazed intently at the water a few hundred metres ahead of the boat. The sea had increased somewhat during the last hour and was running from the south-westward and therefore exactly from ahead, so that we ran the danger of sighting the

mines too late to avoid them, because they disappeared from
sight in the trough of every wave.

Suddenly we all three of us glanced at one another and then
quickly back at the water again. There they were. Heavens,
what masses! Everywhere, as far as the eye could reach, were
the infernal black globes, surrounded by snow-white foam from
the breaking sea. We were so overwhelmed by the quantity of
mines that we started to grouse without stopping.

'Such meanness is unheard of, and they call themselves
Christian seamen – that band of robbers and hypocrites!'

We went at slow speed towards the 'caviare tit-bits', as
Petersen had christened the black-dotted surface of the water
ahead of us. It was our endeavour to steer carefully between
the irregularly distributed mines, keeping a good look-out
ahead to see that we did not get into a cul-de-sac. It was most
important that we should not touch the damned things, as
that would be a very dangerous experiment. Now, with proper
care, we ought to get through safely. We had the good fortune
to have a 'war helmsman' who was not made of paste.

Boatswain's mate Lomann owed his first-rate steering to the
constant practice he had had during the whole of his naval
career. He had been a special 'war-helmsman' ever since he
became a bluejacket, and whenever he committed a crime –
and in times gone by that was no infrequent occurrence – it
was always pleaded in extenuation of his offence 'but he is such
a good helmsman.'

Lomann, who, when he wished, could touch any object floating in the water with the bow of the boat, stood behind the
wheel on top of the conning-tower with his legs apart, grinning
from ear to ear. He always grinned when he was standing at
the helm; but now, when he was the most important man on
board, he beamed to such an extent on account of this honour
and was so inordinately proud of his position, that his small
four-cornered figure gave the impression of studied laziness.

Now we were thrusting right into the minefield. Lomann
puckered up his small grey eyes to such an extent that they
were hardly visible, spat first upon his right hand, and then
contemptuously with a high trajectory towards the first mine

which we had just passed on our port side.

Next he pulled up his leather trousers, which were slipping down, lit his nose-warmer – a clay pipe which was broken off close to the bowl – spat once more into his right hand, and then began to make artistic turns and twists through the lanes, which were dangerously narrow. He was so calm and certain the whole time, as if he had done nothing else all his life except steer U-boats through minefields, that I let him go his own way entirely.

After ten minutes we left the minefield behind us, and we estimated that we had passed eight hundred mines.

We proceeded at high speed towards the second minefield.

CHAPTER X

FOR DEAR LIFE

Now commenced a series of events which was to make this day the richest in experiences of all the days which have been spent by U-boats during their wartime voyages.

Ten forty-two a.m.

A British destroyer was patrolling up and down on the far side of the second minefield. We were obliged therefore to dive quickly and pass through the mines submerged. A highly disagreeable thought!

The destroyer has not seen us. The sea is increasing, the barometer is falling fast, and the sky is becoming covered with black rain-clouds. The visibility of the atmosphere decreases. The sea is rough and covered with patches of white foam. The periscope becomes constantly covered with rolling, white-crested waves, so that I cannot see anything for several seconds at a time. Suddenly we are right amongst the mines. I can only see them when they are very close indeed to us, as the tide has risen and only allows the upper portion of the black spheres to bob up now and again. A timely retreat is out of the question.

We are just running straight on to a mine, in a second we have reached it, and it passes only a few metres from the periscope; at the same time we pass on the other side at a distance of five metres three mines lying close together in a group. This is the Devil's own journey! And the damned destroyer sticks to the other side of the minefield and forces us to continue the infernal passage under water. She has absolutely no consideration for our highly precarious situation. How delighted she would be if we suddenly flew skywards in a cloud of smoke and flame. God in heaven! we nearly gratified her.

Then suddenly IT had struck the periscope with a harsh metallic sound – a sound that, as long as life lasts, I shall never forget. But the mine which I saw quite close astern of us as soon as the periscope was free from water, had had compassion upon us: it merely turned on its axis and did us no harm: perhaps it was old and rotten.

It had been too much for me, though; I experienced the sensations of a would-be suicide who had missed himself. 'Let her go down!' I shouted below to the control-room. 'Go to twenty-five metres.'

Better to go through this hell with closed eyes than constantly to observe one's last moment in front of one, without being able to do anything to help. But suppose that when we were deep down, a mine mooring got hung up on the boat, and the mine was drawn under? . . . but all the same the chances of getting through were greater at twenty-five metres than they were at periscope depth.

'Put on the gramophone,' I ordered, 'and play something cheerful, please!'

In spite of the 'Nice new field-grey uniform' which was soon ringing through the boat, I heard on two occasions an infernal grinding and slipping noise on the outside of the conning-tower – mine moorings which we had touched. At last, after minutes which seemed like hours, we must have got through the mines. I let the boat come up, raised the periscope, and had a look round. Thank God, the air, or, what was much more important, the sea, was clear. The destroyer was a few hundred metres astern of us, and we were certain therefore that we had passed through the pestilent region. Ah, there also is the first buoy – the first one, which marks the small sand-bank. Now the channel becomes narrow, and careful steering and pilotage is necessary. If only the tide were not so strong here. It is continually setting us laterally off our course, and I must be always making allowance for it.

'Helmsman, how far ought we to be from the land?'

The helmsman pulled the chart out of its case, laid the compasses upon it, and then measured the distance on the scale. 'Two and a half miles!'

'Dash it all, and we cannot see anything of it yet! It has become quite impossible to see anything up topsides. It only needed that!'

The patrolling destroyer now came rushing past us on our port side. She was not very far away. I lowered the periscope for a time. Who can picture my horror when I put the periscope up again a few minutes later and found that I could see nothing, absolutely nothing at all! A black rain-cloud was rolling along the water and burst into millions of liquid jets and robbed us of all vision. And this just at the spot at which it was absolutely necessary for me to see something, as the channel became so dangerously narrow. There was only a very narrow passage, about two hundred metres broad, which we must rigidly stick to, as any lateral error to starboard or port would put us on the sand-banks without any doubt. And now nothing to be seen of the buoy which marked the narrow channel, nothing to be seen but the grey, powdery wall of rain. And to cap it all, a strong tide whose strength was unknown! I searched, searched, searched for the buoy. My brow was wet with perspiration, and my agitation made me so hot that the eyepiece of the periscope was continually getting misty from the heat of my head. The helmsman had to keep on wiping the glass with a leather cloth.

'Now we ought to have reached the buoy. I can't see it, helmsman! Good God, what shall we do? This is rotten luck! I don't know what to make of it. And on top of it all that destroyer is lurking behind that accursed wall of rain, and may turn up any moment, like a ghost, right alongside us!'

We did not sight the buoy.

Then the weather began to clear up. The rain became thinner and the visibility improved.

We sighted the land first, then the destroyer, far away on the port hand, heading towards us, and then – then –

All good Spirits take pity on us!

The buoy – our buoy – was on the wrong side! On the starboard side instead of on the port side.

And we! Great God in heaven! We were off our course and running straight on to the sand-bank. We should be on it for certain soon, soon. Too late had the weather cleared up, too late in all probability to avoid a terrible misfortune.

'Hard a-port! Both engines full speed astern!' Nothing else to be done!

Then came the calamity.

A jolt, a shock, a crash – U-202 had grounded. Then we went through a terrible time. The sea, which found no room to spread itself out when it met the shoal, reared on high against the steeply rising sand, towered in a raging precipitous mountain of water, toppled over in surging foam, tore itself once more free, and rushed away with a thunderous roar, only to break asunder again into gurgling, flying, driving foam. All the angry surging seas broke over our poor monster-fish, hurled themselves upon us; in the boisterous joy of destruction, played ball with us, flung us upward and threw us to the ground, so that our steel entrails clattered and trembled.

We had lost all control over the boat. The raging of the breakers became wilder, so that we could hear it through the thick steel plates. Every fresh and furious blow from the sea threw us higher upon the sand. That was our greatest danger. The upper portion of the conning-tower and the bow of the boat were already showing above the water; in a short time the whole boat would be visible above the surface. Then we should be lost and, as a helpless wreck, would make a good target for the destroyer.

Pale and collected, all hands stood at their posts, clinging to the nearest solid object, so that they might not be thrown down by the frantic plunging and rolling of the boat. I looked in turn with frightened staring eyes at the pointer of the depth indicator, and at the merciless raging of the sea, which I could see all around us through the scuttles of the conning-tower. Ah, if it was only the sea that we had to fear, but there, through the foam and spray, coming straight at us like a bull with lowered horns, was the black smoking wretch of a destroyer, looking more merciless than all the perils of the raging storm.

The thought flew through my mind that we must remain submerged, must at all costs keep the boat under water, even at the risk of being dashed to pieces on the bottom. Anything was better than to be forced on to the surface and there perforated at leisure by the English shells.

'Flood the ballast tanks!' I cried down to the control-room. 'Fill all the tanks right up, Engineer; do you understand? We must on no account rise any higher.'

'All the ballast tanks are being flooded,' came back from below.

How quiet it was in the control-room! No word was spoken, no anxious conjectures, no advice, and no questions.

A deep unspeakable depression weighed heavily on me. My poor boat, my poor crew! There they stood unmoved at their posts in the fulfilment of their duty, having expressed their trust in me with every look and word; each one was a hero and still so young and strong. And now, their leader had brought them to the abyss 'twixt life and death; and to me, the only one who realised the hopelessness of our situation, it looked as if the shadow of death was slowly bending deeply down towards us. The destroyer continued to approach us with uncanny certainty. Her sharp bow was pointing exactly towards us. She must soon discover the uncovered portions of our conning-tower and bow, over which the sea was breaking treacherously, and then it would be all up with us. Then a hail of shells would come whizzing past, and the foaming hungry sea would come rushing in upon us through the open sluices.

The flooding of the ballast tanks had had the desired effect. The boat lay heavily on the ground, and offered more resistance to the seas, but although she was no longer thrown any higher up on the shoal, the blows of the sea were of much greater severity on account of the increase in the dead weight. It was a miracle that the boat was not dashed to pieces like glass; and we all looked at each other with astonishment after any particularly heavy blow, surprised that nothing happened beyond the occasional bursting of an electric light with a loud report. 'First-class material,' I could not help thinking to myself. The helmsman, who was looking through the scuttle on the port side over my shoulder at the destroyer, suddenly said in his homely Saxon: 'Ach, why should he see us here? He would never expect to find one of us sitting here in the middle of this storm!'

'Helmsman, child of nature, you old optimist, I shall never forget that word of yours. Great God! if you were only right, that would be absolutely – '

'Well, she is turning away already,' the little man interrupted me, flattening his nose against the glass of the scuttle in order to get a better view.

I got him by the neck and wrenched him away from the scuttle, as the blood rushed to my head.

'What? What do you say? She is turning away? Great heavens above us! in all truth, she is turning away, she is turning, she is always turning farther – she is lying broadside on to us already, she will soon show us her stern, she has turned away, she is going away from us, she has not seen us, she has not seen us! . . .'

I remember being given, when I was a small boy, a most lovable toy spaniel, which I dearly worshipped. He was my constant companion, and even had to sleep at night on a rug next my bed. One lovely summer's day, we were sunning ourselves on the big grass-plot in front of the house, when suddenly an enormous strange boarhound sprang towards my beloved dog and chased him wildly across the grass-plot, thirsting for his blood. The angry hound must soon have caught him, for my poor little pet had only got a start of three strides and was crying pitifully for help. I stood there transfixed with horror and could not say a word. At the last minute the owner appeared and whistled the evil brute off. Then I flew in rapturous bliss to my beloved dog, so narrowly saved, pressed him in my arms, kissed his black nose, and laughed and cried from

sudden joy. .... My feelings were very similar when I saw with
my own eyes the unbelievable happen, as the destroyer steamed
away from us unconscious of our presence. Was it really possible, then, that she had not seen us, when she had been only
eight hundred metres distant from us at the outside, according
to my estimate? Was the helmsman's reasoning really correct,
and had the stupid fellow in the destroyer only searched the
fairway in accordance with Scheme F? 'But,' I thought with an
after-shudder, 'how easily could a chance glance have betrayed
us.'

Beaming with delight, I imparted to the control-room the
unhoped-for turn of luck which our fortunes had undergone
during the last hour. A great weight must have been lifted from
the dauntless souls of the brave men down below.

Then I revealed my plan to the engineer.

'We will remain,' I said down the voice-pipe, 'lying quietly
here until the destroyer has reached the end of her patrol, when
she will be from three to four miles away from us. Then at my
order you must empty all the diving tanks simultaneously, so
that the boat will come off the bottom, and we will get into deep
water at top speed and dive once more.'

A fresh rainstorm, somewhat milder than the first one, was
beating up and favoured our plan. The destroyer was fast dis-
appearing in the mist. Now we could risk it, come to the surface
and thereby escape from the dangers arising from the blows
and buffeting of the storm.

The valves were quickly opened. Directly the boat lifted, the
terrible pounding ceased, the pointer of the depth indicator
rose, and a few seconds later the topsides of the hull broke
through the surface of the water. We were up once more.

'There was the buoy! Full speed ahead!'

We shall soon be there; only another few hundred metres,
and the game is ours. The game, in which the stakes were life
and death, and the playing of which would have turned the
hair on our temples grey had we not all been so young; the
game that had woven a new bond between us, an unbreakable
bond uniting us firmly and formed through sharing in common
the perils of war.

When we had the buoy on the proper side, we plunged once more into the deep cool stream, as happy and fresh as a fish that, after lying on dry ground, finds itself once more surrounded by its own element.

The first and most dangerous portion of our dash through the Witches' Cauldron was now accomplished, although not without tremendous difficulties.

The narrow entrance-gate was passed; our way lay through a wide channel, several miles across, and free from sand-banks or other hindrances to navigation. We bustled along in a new and cheerful temper in the deep spacious waters, whilst we tapped, listened to, and felt our good boat in all quarters, to see whether, after saving her with such difficulty, she had emerged whole and without springing a leak from the steaming storm-kettle. This work made us soon forget the dangers through which we had passed. So long as the nerves were kept at high tension, they had neither the inclination nor the opportunity to brood on what had gone before. Although we had had good luck in getting through the mines and the sand-banks, there was yet a long time to wait for the end of the day, and the principal work lay in front of us still. New and entirely unforeseen surprises were continually following one another throughout this memorable day, so that we felt at last that everything was in league against us.

CHAPTER XI

IN THE ENEMY'S NETS

NEXT we came across trawlers, drifters, and other small craft which tow a steel hawser between every pair, in order to search the channel for submarines. It always happened that at the moment when we cautiously raised the periscope in order to have a quick look all round, we had, as sure as death, a group of these vessels ahead of us, so that we were compelled to dive rapidly to a very great depth in order to avoid the dangerous hawser. When for once it had been possible to make a brief survey, it was thick all round – that is to say, the visibility was bad, and the land, which must have been very near to us on both sides, was completely hidden. At last we had no idea of our position, as the tides in this neighbourhood are quite unreliable, and we had had no mark in sight from which to obtain a fix, since the famous buoy at noon. We were trying to keep to the middle of the channel purely by guesswork, and trusted to our lucky star to guide us aright. At every hour we rose from our safe depth and tried to get our position, returning to the old place again unsatisfied and disappointed on each occasion.

Naturally all the crew had to remain at their diving stations the whole time. At two o'clock the cook went round the boat and issued the small tin basins filled with pea-soup and bacon. His arms were stretched up to us also in the conning-tower, and on the top of his outspread fingers the steaming bowl was enthroned. I perched myself upon the hydrostatic gear between the periscopes, put the plate on my knees and got to work with my spoon. It made me think of the feeding of the beasts at the Zoo. The sweat which collects on the deck during long journeys under water, just as in a dripping stone cavern, was falling on my head and into my food, and the film of oil which was thus deposited on my pea-soup was the sign that it was real U-boat sweat. That is always oily.

At four o'clock I came up once more to periscope depth. A group of vessels was sweeping the channel five hundred metres astern of us; at the same distance on our starboard bow a large French torpedo-boat with four funnels was lying in wait. Nothing was to be seen of the land. I would gladly have blown up the Frenchman, which was an absolutely modern craft, but the great probability of putting the waiting pack of hounds on our trail in this dangerous region made me abstain from so doing.

I must say it was a hard thing at the moment to have to be obliged to forego the shot, and it was with a sad heart that I lowered the periscope and gave the order to descend into the depths.

That was our salvation. Had I remained a few minutes longer at periscope depth, I should not be sitting here today smoking cigarettes and writing down my experiences.

We were diving downwards and the depth indicator showed seventeen metres. Suddenly we all felt as if someone had knocked us on the head with a hammer. Momentarily we lost consciousness, and then we found ourselves lying on the deck or thrown into some corner, with aching heads, shoulders, or other limbs. The whole boat trembled and shook. Were we still alive, or what had happened? Why was it so dark, such a pitch-black night? Ah, the lights had gone out!'

'Have a look at the cut-out!'

'It has blown out!'

'Put in a spare one!'

Suddenly it was day once more. All this took place in a few seconds, much quicker than I can tell it here.

What had happened? Was it not indeed the end of all things for us? Was not the water rushing into the boat somewhere and forcing us down to the bottom? That was a mine, the tremendous frantic detonation of a mine close, close to the boat. And the boat? The result?

From all compartments reports were being made without having to ask for them. 'Bow compartment tight,' 'All well aft,' "All tight in the engine-room,' 'Everything tight!'

Then the boat took an unusual tilt. The bow sank deep down and the stern rose. She made a violent plunge in spite of the fact that the depth-rudders were hard up in the opposite direction.

'Captain,' cried out Gröning, who was working the depth-rudders, 'something is wrong. The boat is no longer answering her helm. We must be caught up somewhere – a hawser, or a net perhaps!'

'Damn it all! It only needed that. Of course we are sitting in the net, and mines are secured to the net over our heads. Ah, it is enough to drive one mad.'

'Attention!' I shouted below; 'we must break through! Work the depth-rudders hard up and down, both engines full speed ahead! Don't let her come up! Keep her down; whatever happens, keep her down; there are mines overhead!'

The engines increased their speed, the boat shot ahead, thrust herself into the net, pushed, twisted, and bored her way in, forced her way downwards, tugged, tore, and tore yet again the steel net into shreds.

'Hurrah, we are through! The boat responds!' shouted Gröning from below. 'The boat is answering her helm once more!'

'Go deeper! Keep at fifty metres,' I commanded. 'This is a dirty neighbourhood. This is absolutely Hell!'

I perched myself once more upon the hydrostatic gear and leant my head upon my hand. It buzzed and whirred like a mill-wheel. I felt as if my forehead, just over my eyes, was being stabbed with needles, and there was a humming in my ears, so that I had to stop them with my fingers. 'That is indeed a dirty neighbourhood,' I repeated softly to myself, 'and we were only saved by a stroke of luck, by that wonderful good luck which attended us.' It was some time before my aching head was in a fit condition to sort things out into any order. Yes, it had been pure joss which made us go down to a greater depth at the right moment. We were at a depth of seventeen metres at the time of the explosion when our bow struck the net. The more I thought about it all, the clearer I got the hang of things. By blundering into the nets, we had aroused their wrath, and had brought the firing-gear of the mines into action. These mines were secured in the nets at a depth at which U-boats usually travel. Had we attempted to attack the torpedo-boat, or had we remained for any other reasons for a short time at peri-scope depth, we should have entered the nets in the manner desired by the enemy – that is to say, the mines would have exploded alongside us or underneath us. As it was, the mine had exploded above us and had expended all its energy in the direction of least resistance – that is to say, upwards – without causing us any more damage than a terrible fright, and perhaps a few beauty spots on the thin tin portions of the upper works.

It was certain that the exulting Frenchman, who had been stationed close to the nets on the look-out and who had doubt-less seen the explosion and gloated over our destruction, was now informing the whole world by wireless telegraphy:

'Hostile submarine destroyed by a mine explosion in the barrier nets.'

Ah, how gladly would we give him that pleasure, if only he would leave us in peace in the future, as we had all had enough of the first encounter.

CHAPTER XII

HUNTED FOR MANY HOURS

THE trials of the day were not over yet by a long way.

The next to appear was Krüger, the engineer officer, standing with a worried look on the ladder leading to the conning-tower.

'Captain, we must have got something foul of the propellers,' he announced. 'We are using double the normal amount of electric power. I think that a bit of the net is wound round the propellers, as the vibration of the motors is heavy and the battery power is falling rapidly.'

Oh dear, now this worry to add to all the others! We had used up a lot of our battery power as it was, because on two occasions we had had to go at full speed, and that eats rapidly into the reserve.

'How long can we manage to go on, Krüger?'

The engineer made a calculation in his notebook and shrugged his shoulders thoughtfully.

'If the vibration does not increase, we can still continue for a couple of hours. It would be better, in any case, to reduce speed a bit.'

I thought it over. In an hour's time, the tide would turn and run against us. We should not get over the ground very quickly then. No matter; it would soon be dark, and then we might perhaps risk coming to the surface. In all probability the enemy was under the impression that we had been destroyed and would keep a less vigilant look-out.

'Very good,' I said to the engineer; 'I will stop one motor. We must go on in any case, as it is impossible to lie on the bottom on account of the great depth of water.'

We stopped one motor, as I had arranged, and proceeded at a very slow speed.

We went up to have a look round punctually at five o'clock. The French torpedo-boat was following exactly in our wake, about two hundred metres away.

'What ho!' I said to the helmsman, as I bit my under-lip nervously, 'it rather looks as if she was following us.'

'It must be by accident,' said our unshakable optimist.

We dived down again, and came up this time half an hour later.

The torpedo-boat was coming along in our wake, just as she had been at five o'clock, at a distance of two hundred metres.

'If that is an accident, helmsman, then it is a very, very extraordinary one.'

When I had another look round at six o'clock, the Frenchman was exactly the same distance astern.

'Devil take her, that is no accident! I'll be hanged if that is an accident. That is intention, angry threatening intention. It is a new and frightful peril. We are being followed!'

Something was the matter with us; the enemy must have some trail that enabled her to follow us, even when we were travelling at a great depth. What could it be?

I thought hard and tortured my poor brain in trying to find the answer, but without success. The only thing that I could think of was that the mine explosion might have caused a leak in one of the oil-tanks, and that the escaping oil was leaving a broad line on the surface of the water behind us and thus giving

us away. Or could it be a coincidence after all, caused by
slow speed over the ground with the tide against us, and
Frenchman was steering the same course and tooling along
behind us unwittingly? It was essential that I should be certain
of the reason, and to find it out I must perforce run both motors
again, in spite of the great expenditure of power.

I gave orders to dive deep, altered course four points to port
and ran both motors at high speed. If the destroyer was really
able to see something of us, she would still follow us, although
we had altered course and were going four times as fast as
before. If, on the other hand, she saw nothing of us, then we
should shake her off by our alterations in course and speed.

When the clock showed half-past seven, I ventured to take a
cautious peep through the periscope, and I saw, just as I had at
five o'clock, at five-thirty, and at six o'clock, the Frenchman
astern of us, having made a similar increase of speed and alter-
ation in course to our own.

Now I knew for certain. All doubts had vanished. We were
both seen and followed. The Frenchman's wireless telegraphy
calls would soon put other tracking hounds upon our trail.
Then the great hunt would begin, Our batteries were almost
run down, and the water was a hundred metres deep, so that we
could not go and lie on the bottom.

'A nice prospect; things may get lively!' I muttered to myself.
To the helmsman and the control-room I said, on the contrary,
in a loud voice, so that all hands could hear: 'There now, she
has gone. I said all along that it was only a fluke.'

My object was to keep up the spirits of the crew, as I could
feel, myself, how much the long day with all its surprises had
got upon my own nerves.

In the plan which I had formed I was counting upon the darkness which would shortly overtake us and upon the battery
lasting out, with the most sparing use of power, until we
reached a certain spot, which I had selected after a careful
study of the chart. We maintained our previous course for
another half-hour, and then, when it must have been quite
dark overhead, we made a sharp turn to starboard of more than
eight points, and shaped course for a spot on the coast where

would enable us to lie on the bottom, to get
...ntil the enemy's activities had abated. That
...owards morning, I thought to myself, and
... south-westerly gale became worse, a methodical
...ith the heavy sweeps would become more difficult. The
...tion which I had chosen for our couch was not exactly a
nice one, as, unlike the one in the North Sea chart with its
plentiful and ever-welcome abbreviation for the nature of the
bottom, 'Sd' – Sand; here I found marked all over the chart of
this locality the much-dreaded abbreviation 'Fls.' – that stands
for rock.

However, we had no choice in the matter; and even Satan
himself is known to eat flies in extremity, although usually he is
reported to exist on better fare. We did not come up any more,
as it was dark overhead, but travelled at slow speed at a great
depth without interruption. We should reach our resting-place
towards midnight, according to my calculations. Our store of
electrical power ought to last until then. Krüger made calculation after calculation, and always arrived at the same
result, that it ought just to last out. Until nine o'clock we
frequently heard the noise of the propellers of our sleuth-
hounds, but from that hour onwards everything was quiet overhead, and I breathed a deep and heartfelt sigh of relief. They
appeared to have lost our trail. It was possible to feel quite
comfortable once more, and I perched myself on the ladderway
leading to the control-room, and ate bread and butter from a
large plate, and drank hot tea, with the officers and men.
Twelve o'clock came, and still we had not touched bottom.
What if the calculations of our position were incorrect? This
would be quite possible with the strong tide and the slow speed
we had been making.

Half-past twelve. No bottom. The engineer shifted nervously
from one foot to the other and put out one electric light after
another, in order to save the power. The electric radiators had
long ago been extinguished for the same reason, and we were
freezing miserably in the damp cellar-like temperature of the
boat.

There, at five minutes to one, we felt a slight shock, and the motors were stopped and reversed in order to reduce the speed; then another shock, and we flooded the ballast tanks and rested upon the bottom.

Thank God that we had reached it! Now we could await the morning and rest.

Rest indeed! Who said rest? Much as we all needed it, very little were we to see of it. Anyone who thought that we were going to have a few hours' rest found himself bitterly disillusioned; for he must have forgotten that our bed was a rockbed, that the tide turned at two o'clock in the night, and that overhead the south-west wind howled and the sea raged.

It was quite all right at first down below on the rocky bottom, but very soon – that was when the tide turned – it became uncomfortable. It was no longer a case of rolling and gentle bumping, as it had been in the North Sea, even when there was a gale; now it was a series of crashing and shattering blows, as we were thrown violently upwards and hurled from one rocky patch to another, so that we looked at one another in perplexity and asked, 'Will she stand it?'

Sometimes it sounded as if huge stones were being rolled across the boat's deck and the diving tanks, and then again the boat would drop three or four metres deeper with a crash, and the pointer on the depth indicator never had any rest. It oscillated between depths of twenty-two and thirty-eight metres for the two hours during which we had to stand this hellish din.

At last, towards four o'clock in the morning, it became too much for us. A few rivets were already beginning to leak, and in any case sleep was out of the question, as our nerves were quite incapable of standing the tossing and clattering any longer. We therefore said good-bye to the bottom and rose to the surface.

As I opened the conning-tower hatch and felt the cold fresh night air beating upon me, I had a remarkable sensation. I felt as if we had been ages long beneath the ground, and had been having a long deep dream. The portals of the underworld had opened like Hörselberg's magic doors, only it was from Neptune and not from Venus that we had escaped after a thousand difficulties. For twenty hours without interruption he had held us fast in his kingdom, and had put us on the rack and tortured us, so that the hours had seemed like years.

The spell passed away as quickly as it had come, for there is no time for dreaming with us. As was only to be expected, the storm had not diminished, but, on the contrary, was blowing with unabated force from the open sea, and driving in front of it a yelping surging pack of high-crested waves. We were all soaked through on top of the conning-tower in a very short time, but we did not mind this small inconvenience, and noted with satisfaction that the water was much warmer here than it had been up in the North Sea. This made us realise that the trials we had undergone in the long hours just past, had brought us, in spite of our wanderings, a good deal nearer our destination. It was the Gulf Stream which surrounded us, and whose warmth can be appreciated only in this neighbourhood, on account of the compression it receives between the two coasts which are close together.

It was a pitch-dark night. Right astern of us, two lights, one white and the other red, were flashing, and made it easy for us to fix our present position. Not an enemy was in view. They had apparently given up the search as hopeless. Can you imagine what a sigh of relief we gave? And how confidence in the further success of our trip rose anew in our hearts, when we could say to ourselves at last that the dangers of the passage through the narrow waters, which had proved to be so much greater than we had anticipated, were overcome and left behind us?

Quickly now we recharged our empty batteries, so as to be ready for any conceivable emergency that might come. With the remaining surface engine we sought the open sea, away from the inhospitable coast, so as to gain time in which to breathe some fresh air and rest our nerves.

When the day began to dawn, we were a good twenty miles out to sea, and had recovered a sufficient reserve of electric power to enable us to go under water for several hours if necessary.

With the slow and timid approach of daylight a new surprise awaited us.

Gröning, who was looking ahead by chance to where the outline of a hull could just be seen, beginning to detach itself from the darkness of the night, seized me suddenly by the arm, contrary to all the rules of etiquette, and pointed with his free arm towards the bow, with eyes and mouth wide open, as if he had seen a ghost.

'Look! what is that?'

I got up, leaned forward, and followed with my eyes the direction indicated by his hand.

'Good gracious!' With one stride I reached the foremost edge of the conning-tower platform in order to get a better view. The whole deck of the boat from the conning-tower right forward to the stem appeared in the half-light of the early morning to be divided into large regular squares, through which a thick dark Something was woven in long serpentine lines. The side of one of the squares was lying close to me, and I bent down and got hold of it, and found that I was holding in my hand a steel wire rope as thick as my finger.

A net! The thought shot through my head. Why, of course!

'We have got the net lying on top of us,' I shouted back to Gröning against the storm; 'the whole boat is covered with it, the remains of yesterday afternoon's net. Get hold of the wire cutters and a hammer and chisel. We must set to work and cut the net away as soon as it is daylight.'

And the thick dark snake which was threaded through the meshes? What was that doing there? It climbed up the starboard side of the boat, wound its way over the forward deck, ran back to port past the conning-tower on its way astern and disappeared into the dawn.

We had not got long to wait before knowing what the snake was, and this realisation caused a ray of bright sunshine to illuminate my memory. Suddenly everything became clear to me. The veil of mystery which had enveloped the uncanny and obstinate tracking of our path was rent like mist when the wind disperses it, and clear and distinct in front of my eyes lay revealed the drama, as it must have been enacted on the surface of the water after the explosion of the mine. A slight shiver started at my wet scarf and ran down my back when I thought how easy it had been made for the destroyer to follow our track.

The snake, which we could follow in all its windings as soon as it became light, was a gigantic float, which was used to support the heavy steel net.

It was made of a light cork-like material, and was thicker than a man's arm and of a shiny light-brown colour. It could be seen from a great distance, and was towing on the surface of the water fully two hundred metres astern of us, where it appeared as a much-twisted and brightly shining tail. This tail, which we were dragging along behind us, accounted for the dogging of our footsteps which had appeared so mysterious. When we tore through the nets at our full speed, a long length of the float had remained entangled in the meshes of the big portion of the nets which had been left lying on us, and had thus been dragged along behind us.

Thanks to the extreme buoyancy of the material of which it was composed, the end of the long tail had remained on the surface of the water the whole time, even when we were travelling at a great depth. The Frenchman, whose attention had been drawn to us by the column of water thrown up by the mine explosion, had sighted our tail, and had followed this distinct guide without much difficulty, in spite of all the turns we had made. The only thing I could not understand, and cannot to this day, was why the fellow had not got us, with such a lovely point of aim. Later on, when it became dark, and we made the big turn, the destroyer had lost our track, as the tail was no longer visible.

The cutting-away of the heavy steel net was a splendid piece of work on the part of our brave sailors. The sea towered on high and broke foaming over the low narrow deck, as if angered by the unusual resistance to the freedom of its raging which it encountered in the steel plating of the tiny nut-shell. The crew stood breast-high in the white breaking foam and had to summon all their strength to withstand the wrath of the onslaught. I stood on the top of the conning-tower like a cat on hot bricks, holding the lifebuoy in my hand ready to throw, and watching with anxious eyes every movement of my men, who were working in great danger to their lives.

Everything went well, and at the end of an hour, which had been most exciting for everyone, we were freed from the last obstruction. Wire-cutters, hammer, chisel, and six soaked and dripping seamen disappeared into the conning-tower, and each one of the six held tightly in his bare fist a rusty little bit of net in memory of our 14th of April.

CHAPTER XIII

ENGLAND'S RESPECT FOR THE RED CROSS

THE sun rose as if nothing had happened. He beamed from the eastern horizon with the most cheerful face in the world, and twinkled at us in a friendly fashion across France as if to say, 'I am neutral, I am neutral.' However, as he rose higher and sent his morning greeting across to the coast of England, he crept with a shudder behind some dense clouds. What was the matter with him? What had spoilt his pleasure, and prevented him from beaming on the young morning? What was there over there that so much offended his neutral soul?

A ship came steaming along. Thick black smoke-clouds curled astern of her and lay heavily on the water. Two tall thin masts, two funnels raking slightly aft, and a light hull with a high bridge.

'A funny sort of ship,' we remarked, as we dived under water.

When, shortly afterwards, we could see the ship right down to the water-line, we discovered through the periscope the disappointing fact that she was a hospital ship. The snow-white colour, the broad green bands running from bow to stern, and the large red crosses painted on her side and flying from her masthead, made it a certainty. I was just about to turn away, as an attack upon a ship rendered sacred by the Red Cross was naturally unthinkable, when my eye was horrified by something I could scarcely believe. I called Gröning to the periscope, so that he could make sure that I had not been mistaken. No, my sight had not deceived me; and I had another look, and confirmed the greatest scandal that the light of the world has ever seen. No wonder the sun had hidden himself, to avoid such a scorning and deriding of all human rights. No, a respectable neutral sun does not shine on such spectacles. He leaves that to the moon, and even she objects.

The ship with the sacred flag of purity and human mercy was laden with guns right fore and aft, and an army of soldiers and horses was packed between the guns and their mountings. Under the protection of the colours and flags thus shamelessly misused, the transport-hospital-ship was proceeding towards the scene of war in the full light of day without any escort.

'Band of swine,' said Gröning as he surrendered the periscope to me once more.

'And what a pity that we cannot get up to them,' I said angrily, stamping my foot on the steel deck plating of the conning-tower so that it rattled. 'I would gladly have wiped that one out – mean, hypocritical brutes! – but it cannot be helped; she is too far away and going too fast for us to be able to cut her off.'

We naturally had a try at it, and went after her at full speed for a long time, until the distance between us became even greater, and with empty batteries we had to give up the hopeless chase. Then we turned away, storming and swearing, and came to the surface shortly afterwards.

CHAPTER XIV

A MERRY HUNT

It was an unpleasant feeling to be lying with empty batteries again after such a short time, only able to hobble along like a lame horse. This state of affairs had to be put an end to. We took no notice therefore of anything else, but sought the open sea and spent many hours in storing power in our accumulator batteries.

Just as we had finished doing this, a perky trawler came and chased us. We none of us had the least desire to go under water again, as the sun was shining so divinely, and the weather was becoming milder with the warmth of spring, with every hour that we got farther south. As the propellers, which had run so reluctantly yesterday, by reason of the fragments of net which had got entangled with them, were now clear and running easily once more, we were enabled to take advantage of the great power and high revolutions developed by our heavy oil engines to get our speed again, so we took on the race and started off laughing and in high spirits to try and beat the trawler. Ah, that was a merry hunt! We might have been only just out of dock, so sharply and quickly did the boat cut through the waves. We were enveloped in a cloak of flying spray resembling a fluttering silver mane, which hung for a second in the air in a thousand sunlit drops and then came splashing down right amongst the sunburnt, laughing faces. What did it matter if we did get wet?

We turned our leather-coated backs on our salt companions with indifference, and looked happily astern to where, at a great distance, the smoking, puffing trawler was pounding along behind us.

'No fear; she won't get us,' I said to Engineer Krüger, who had come up into the conning-tower to ask if our speed was sufficient or if he should drive the engines still faster. 'You can leave them running quietly, just as before, Engineer; that is quite good enough; the distance is increasing visibly.'

Our pursuer, who had apparently tumbled to the fact that she could not overtake us, now tried to annoy us by other means. We suddenly heard a report from over in her direction and a brown cloud of smoke enveloped the small vessel for a short space. Then a small shell splashed in the sea at least a thousand metres short, and a column of water no higher than a three-year-old fir tree shot up in the air.

We all laughed heartily. 'Such a plum-thrower! Trying to impress us with his box of toys. Absolutely ridiculous!'

'That is a bit of cheek,' Petersen groused, feeling offended in his capacity of gunnery officer. 'We can't lie down under that. May I reply, Captain?' He turned towards me with sparkling eyes.

'All right, Petersen, you may if you want to. But only three shots, mind. In any case you won't hit her at this range, and our shells are too precious to waste!'

Petersen sprang to the gun, beaming with joy, trained it round, laid it at high elevation, and fired, being frequently up to his waist in water.

'Short and to the right!' I shouted to him, after I had observed the column of water through my binoculars. The second shot fell in unmistakable proximity to the trawler.

'Good shot,' I shouted from the conning-tower and winked at Petersen.

Then it became too hot for the pursuer. She turned sharp round and went off in the opposite direction. But we were seized in our turn with the lust of the hunter. We turned the tables on her and pursued the fleeing pursuer.

Now go ahead, engines, and show what you can do; fly away, shells, our best wishes attend you!

Shot after shot fled thundering from the muzzle. The distance was great and we had to give the gun almost its extreme elevation in order to get anywhere near the mark. The first shots all fell either to one side or short, but finally, at the eighth round, we succeeded in getting a hit. Tremendous hurrahs greeted the dark-brown cloud-burst which attended the impact of the shell on the trawler. Her small gun replied uselessly with shell after shell which fell nowhere near us. On our side one hit followed another on the enemy ship; and we saw that she had already a heavy list to port, and were hoping to administer the death-blow to her when behind her and to left and right the outlines of three of her consorts appeared, approaching at high speed. There was nothing left for us but to turn round, to avoid being surrounded, for too many dogs are death to the hare.

CHAPTER XV

THE LOVABLE
FRENCHMAN

WE submerged early in the evening in order to spend the night in the security of the deep. We were thoroughly tired out, as we had all gone through a day's work of thirty-eight hours' duration, and felt the great relaxation of nerve tension now that we had reached a time of comparative quiet. This relaxation was soon made even more apparent by reason that we were unable to get off to sleep properly, and when sleep did come eventually, it was filled with uneasy dreams. Personally, I lay long awake, and heard through the open doors, in the deathly stillness of the underwater world, the crew tossing about restlessly in their bunks, and talking and shouting in their dreams, just as if we were in a parrot's cage instead of in a submarine. I also, in my dreams of this night, lived over once again most of the events of the past hours, only the curious thing was that I was never the fish but always the fisherman on the surface, and I was helping the torpedo-boat eagerly to try and catch my own U-boat. When I woke up I could not find my way back to reality, and kept on seeing over and over again

quite distinctly before my eyes the black-bearded countenance
of the French captain, as, with the lust of destruction shining in
his small dark eyes, he said: *'Diable, il faut attraper la canaille!'*
('Deuce take it, we must catch the rascal!')

When we rose to the surface in the morning, we were greeted
by a glorious blue sky and a calm sea. The wind had not only
gone down considerably during the night, but had veered as
well, so that it was now blowing off the land, and was unable
therefore to disturb the sea to any great extent. Having break-
fasted well, we sat on the top of the conning-tower, refreshed
and in the best of tempers, rejoicing in the lovely day and puffing one cigarette after another in the warm spring air. We had
reached overnight the locality in which we contemplated remaining for some time in order to wage war against the cargo
ships which were flourishing in this neighbourhood. With this
object we cruised backwards and forwards on various courses,
with guns loaded and eyes wide open, so as not to miss any
opportunity of damaging the enemy's trade.

Shortly before midday, the first hostile vessel arose on the
southern horizon. It was a sailing ship, a big fully rigged and
deeply laden vessel, which was steering close-hauled towards
the French coast. In majestic calm, heeling slightly to the wind
pressure, the magnificent ship approached. Her snow-white
sails reflected the sun's rays, and stood sharply out from the
deep blue of the heavens, like the wings of a lightly swooping
giant gull. Her light-grey hull rested gently on the water as she
thrust her way, with foaming bow-wave, through the well-
trusted element. With a cheer we rushed at our prize. Already,
when still a long way off, the coloured pendants and little flags
which meant 'Abandon ship at once' were fluttering overhead.

Clear and concise, brightly illuminated by the sun, shone the
order from our little ship to the huge heavily laden vessel we
were approaching, and the colours of the German war ensign,
which was flaunted on the flagstaff abaft the conning-tower, left
no doubt as to the bitter earnestness of the command.

Had they got no signal-book, or did they not wish to understand? Ah yes, now a flag was being hoisted at the tall mast of
the sailing ship. The wind caught it, and carried it out, and

there, proud and plain, fluttered the French tricolour. The flag remained stationary when it was half-mast high – the signal for help! (The ensign hoisted at half-mast was the cry for assistance from a ship being chased.) So they had understood our order all right, and were calling for help before obeying it. Wait, my little friend, we will soon have that down!

'Hoist the signal: "Stop at once, or I fire!" ' The new signal flew aloft. Look out, Frenchman, this is no longer a joke, and soon the little grey beast which is moving round you will bite.

'We will give him three minutes in which to think over the situation, and then shoot at his masts,' I shouted to Petersen, who was standing at the gun trembling with excitement.

Watch in hand, I counted three full minutes. The sailing ship behaved just as if we did not exist and held to her course.

'What a shame,' I muttered to myself, and put my watch away. Then I shouted out loud, so that I could be heard all over the boat, 'Open fire!'

Rrrrroms! thundered the gun, making our ears buzz as the shell leapt out and, splitting and crashing, rent a great hole in the upper rigging of the ship. It struck the fore yard, and cracked and tore the big spar right through, so that it came down with a run, bringing the sails with it.

The result was instantaneous. The red and white pendant, which means in the International Code Signal book 'Signal understood', flew aloft. The sailors, who had collected in a bunch on the after deck and were looking at us with excited curiosity, separated at an order from the captain, and ran to their stations for working ship: long-drawn-out orders, given in the sing-song tone of the French language, were heard, the top-gallant sails and royals came down with a run, and the courses and top-sails were braced aback. The ship was checked and gradually lost her way. Boats were swung out and cleared away, men ran about in cork jackets, and vast excitement was visible wherever you looked.

We went to windward of the ship and shouted to the captain to hurry up. We told him we could give him ten minutes more to clear out, and then his ship would be torpedoed. Down below, in the bow compartment where the torpedo-tubes were situated and the shining torpedoes lay, feverish activity had reigned from the moment when the alarm signal had resounded through the boat on sighting the enemy merchant ship. There is little room there – in fact it is extremely narrow – and a particularly accomplished and especially skilful *personnel* is required, to know their way about amongst the confused mass of pipes, valves, and pumps. The officers' mess, which occupies the after part of the torpedo space, and which, for all ordinary and reasonable purposes, is quite homely and comfortable, was transformed in a second into a bare unlivable space.

Active hands set to work, drew the oil-smeared curtains across the officers' bunks, and clapped the small table and the four camp-stools together and put them in a corner. That disposed of all the luxury in the room, and a clear space was made for the handling of the torpedoes.

Schweckerle, the mate of the bow compartment, was a real father to his torpedoes. He loved them as if they were his children, and he was oiling, greasing, and testing them the whole day long, and his affection for his carefully tended treasures knew no bounds. The others said of him that he mourned each of his charges which he had to give up, and unkind tongues went even further and affirmed that they had once heard him swearing aloud in his bunk because he had had to part with several torpedoes at once on the previous day. One thing at any rate was true, for I had observed it myself, and that was that when a torpedo had run badly for some unknown reason and missed its target, he went about broken-hearted for several days and eating nothing at all.

This faithful torpedo-soul was, needless to say, anxious once more to save his children, and had withdrawn 'Brisk' and 'Quick Devil' (thus were the first two torpedoes in the row christened) from the tubes before he received the order through the voice-pipe, 'Get the first tube ready to fire!'

Therefore it was 'Quick Devil's' turn. Good! Hurry up now!

Schweckerle was in his element, and when Schweckerle's commanding voice was heard the torpedo-tube's crew jumped about as if the devil were behind them.

'You here, you there, you this, you that forward, hurry,

buck up! Get the grease-pot and grease that! That is right, that is enough! Now in with her, altogether, launch forward, shove will you! Shove handsomely – handsomely! Stop!'

A softly murmured final admonition to the torpedo as it disappeared into the tube, a last leave-taking look and Schweckerle slammed the heavy door behind it with a loud clang. 'Quick Devil' was ready to be fired.

Shortly afterwards I was aware of this on top of the conning-tower, but the time was not yet come. Only a small portion of the ten minutes' respite had elapsed. We had time enough to make a closer inspection of the sailing ship before we sent her to the bottom. She was a big modern ship built of steel and was rigged with every imaginable device of modern times. I guessed that she could carry from three to four thousand tons cargo. Doubtless she came from afar, for ships of that size and description were not used for coastal work. Of what did her cargo consist?

Then the Frenchmen got into their boats and left the ship. The last boat came to grief as it was being lowered, and stood on end, so that all the crew fell into the water, but another boat was quickly on the spot, and the swimmers were fished out. When everyone was in safety, I turned the bow of our boat towards the sailing ship lying quietly on the water, and fired the torpedo from the first tube at a distance of a few hundred metres.

Poor Schweckerle – there it goes! But it is running well, Schweckerle, absolutely as straight as a die. Bravo, Schweckerle!

The Frenchmen in the boats, who had come quite close up to us, because they thought that this was the safest position, shouted with fright as the detonation followed, and the column of water shot up high above the mastheads.

'Oh, mon Dieu, mon Dieu, notre pauvre vaisseau!' (O God, our poor ship.')

Poor devils, I could not help thinking, I can understand your grief on account of your fine, good ship. But why don't you remain at home? Why do you go to sea, when you know what awaits you? Why do you, or your Government, compel us to sink your ships wherever we meet them? Must we wait until our wives and children are starving, and must we allow our bread-basket to be hung even higher by you, without defending ourselves?

You began it; you must bear the consequences. If you stop first of all your inhuman method of waging war, then we will gladly leave your sailing vessels to sail in peace, and your harm-lessly laden ships to proceed on their way. You wanted war to the knife – well, you shall have it.

The sailing ship sank quickly. First the stern disappeared into the waves, then she lay so far over on her side that the gunwale almost touched the water, and the bright red bottom was visible, and finally, after the compression of the air in the foremost hold had burst the scuttles, and in its release had thrown out a cloud of maize, the whole proud ship went hurt-ling down into the deep. Gurgling, the sea rushed inwards, and as it closed in foaming breakers, it formed a brief and transitory grave-stone over the sunken ship. The captain came on board. Not for a moment did he forget to be the bowing polite French-man. He swung himself elegantly up on to the top of the conning-tower, smiled his most engaging boulevard smile, and permitted himself to hand over the ship's papers to *monsieur le capitaine* with a gracious bow. In return I offered him, with my most friendly Germanic look, a cigarette, which he accepted with a smile as if he had been my best friend for years. He answered in the most willing manner all questions as to where and whence he was bound, and produced, unasked-for, the bill of lading, to show us what a valuable catch we had made. It appeared to be most astonishing to him that we should be cruis-ing about here in our little nutshell, and he showed no dis-inclination to accompany us on our piratical voyage, as he had the kindness to call it. When I allowed myself to ask him the modest question why he had not answered my two first signals to stop and to abandon ship, he appeared as innocent as a new-born babe, and declared, with his southern vivacity, that he had seen absolutely no signal at all. Indeed, he went so far as to declare that he had not seen any ship at all until the shells went past him. He met my objection that his last statement was ren-dered rather difficult to believe by the signal for help which he had hoisted long before, with wonderful nonchalance, and hastened to give the conversation another turn in a very artful manner. This dexterous Frenchman was not to be caught, and even when I had him in the pincers, where another could not have escaped in any direction, he slipped out like an eel with remarkable friendliness.

I had noticed how well dressed the men in the boats were, and how cleanly washed and shaved they appeared to be. I, a barbarian, did not want to be behindhand in friendliness, so I complimented the captain on the smart appearance of his crew.

That started him off whining in a new and hitherto unused tone of voice:

'Ah, the poor boys,' he lamented, 'they have not always looked like that on this long journey; they have spent the whole morning in cleaning and scrubbing themselves, because they were in hopes of getting on shore this evening. Look here, *mon Capitaine*,' as he threw open the ship's log book, 'we sailed from Saigon on the 23rd of January; we have traversed half the world, and now, a few hours before reaching our destination, fate overtakes us. Ah, it is a tragedy, a tragedy!'

I comforted him as well as I could, and promised to do my best to procure for him and his crew even yet the hoped-for landing. Then I offered him a cigarette once more as a parting gift, shook him warmly by the hand, and let him leave the ship. We had arranged that I would tow the boats toward the land until I sighted a fresh prize; and then they must see how they could get along alone.

Shortly after two o'clock this came about, as we sighted some mastheads in the distance with white sails spread on yards.

We therefore cast off the two boats, wished them a good journey, and turned round towards our fresh victim.

Schweckerle had to get 'Rapid' ready.

CHAPTER XVI

THE ENGLISH BULL-DOG AND OTHER THINGS

As we drew nearer, we discovered something which made us suspicious. We had ascertained that the ship which was approaching was a large three-masted fully rigged ship, very similar in type to the one we had sunk shortly before. What made us suspicious, however, and aroused our deepest mistrust was the fact that from time to time we saw distinctly, either between or abaft the sails, black smoke-clouds, which were being emitted apparently in the near neighbourhood of the sailing ship. That was suspicious, and continued to remain so.

Anything which you cannot explain, you look at with suspicion. In order to comply with this fully established U-boat maxim, we, as cautious people, proceeded to keep away a bit, in order to pass the mysterious ship at a greater distance. We had heard too much of so-called U-boat traps, to act as the bull does with the red rag, and charge at anything ahead of us without having a look first. What if behind the high hull of the sailing ship, which acted as a decoy-bird, a small fast torpedo-boat should be in hiding, ready to spring on us, like lightning from a serene sky? No, we had to make certain, first of all, with whom we had to deal.

Soon the situation became clear. Two hundred metres ahead of the sailing ship a short powerful sea-going tug was towing the ship astern by means of a large hawser, in order to increase her speed.

There was nothing else suspicious hereabouts. It was often the custom of sailing ships to allow themselves to be towed for the last fifty miles, so as to arrive before evening, and thus to save a whole day. For this reason the steam-tugs of the big tug associations went far afield to offer their highly paid services.

Ah, we thought, this is far from being a danger, but, on the contrary, a really favourable opportunity for destroying a ship and being enabled at the same time to send her crew safely to land; for we never allowed this object to remain unconsidered when it could be attained in conjunction with our duty.

I rubbed my hands together with satisfaction.

'We will let the crew of the sailing ship go aboard the tug and send them home. Perhaps they will meet their shipwrecked brethren from our first prize and take them along too.'

With that we altered course towards the tug and went at high speed. Then we circled carefully round the prize in order to make certain that no hidden gun should send us suddenly a surprise greeting. We paid particular attention to the tug through our glasses, as she, who was employed daily in and around these waters in her duties as adviser to homeward-bound ships, was more likely to be armed than was the sailing ship, coming from distant parts. We spotted nothing suspicious. All right, go ahead! We shot up from astern and then reduced speed, and kept within hail of the tug on a parallel course. Gröning, Petersen, boatswain's mate Lomann, and a sailor were with me on top of the conning-tower.

The tug was flying the English flag, and therefore I got hold of the megaphone kept for the English and shouted with all the strength of my lungs:

'Take the crew over!'

I pointed towards the sailing ship with my left arm at the same time, in order to illustrate my words.

The master of the small *Bull-dog*, as Petersen liked to call the stout little tug, took his briar pipe out of his mouth and spat into the water over the bridge rails, against which he was leaning.

Apart from that he did not take any further notice of us, except possibly for a few sly cunning glances from under the shelter of his gilt-embroidered cap. I took it that he must be hard of hearing, and I placed the boat a few metres closer to him.

'Take the crew over,' I shouted to him anew, and let all the others on the conning-tower shout with me.

The wind had freshened during the last hours, and the sea had become so rough that the water was coming right over the deck and rendered the employment of the guns out of the question – the guns' crews would have been swept over the side inevitably. We were unable, therefore, to give our repeated order to take over the crew of the sailing ship the support which we should have liked to. But we knew how to help ourselves. As the master of the *Bull-dog* continued to show no inclination to carry out our oft-repeated order, which he doubtless understood, I sent below for a rifle and shot a whistling bullet past the head of the thick-skulled fellow. The Englishman seemed to understand this language better. He stepped back from the bridge rails, blew a shrill blast on a mouth-whistle, and shouted loud curt orders to the hurrying crew. Then he turned for the first time fully towards us, put his hand to his cap in brief salutation, and then raised his right arm straight up into the air. That meant, according to the international seamen's language: 'I have understood and I agree.'

The crew of the *Bull-dog*, which was in reality called the *Ormea*, had in the meantime slipped the tow-rope of the sailing ship and were standing round about the deck with their hands in their trouser-pockets in thoughtful curiosity. The captain went to the engine telegraph and put it to 'Ahead'.

'Aha,' we thought, 'now he is going to turn round and go alongside the sailing ship.'

What then took place was the work of a few seconds. When the *Ormea* had got up speed, she suddenly turned sharply to starboard towards us, instead of to port, which would have been her nearest way. At the same time the engine telegraph flew to 'Full speed ahead' under the hand of the captain, and the strongly built and speedy tug shot ahead with high foaming bow-wave.

We had naturally been closely watching every movement over there and had not dreamt of any hostile intention until the moment when the tug stopped turning and came straight at us. Then we suddenly realised our terrible danger.

'The fellow must be mad,' I cried out; 'he is trying to ram us! Both engines full speed ahead! Hard a-port!'

But it appeared as if we had realised our danger too late. The tug had the advantage of us in having got her speed up, and she came rushing and smoking on us like a raging bull-dog. The distance between the two ships, which had been a good two hundred metres to begin with, decreased with great rapidity. Now the foaming bow was barely fifty metres away from us.

Our hair stood on end underneath our caps.

'Pistols up – rifles!' I shouted down into the conning-tower. The weapons, which were always kept fully loaded hanging on the conning-tower wall, were quickly handed up, and we opened a tremendously rapid fire on the snorting enemy, who was always coming nearer and nearer. I could see plainly the captain's cunning watery-blue eyes shining fiendishly, and I witnessed the pleasure depicted on his grinning face. Devil take him! he had good cause to rejoice. He would get us, he was bound to get us, for he was faster than we were and had the better position. Always nearer and nearer came the moment when the clumsy iron bow would bore its way into our side, and the nearer our Fate approached, the wilder and the more excitedly beat our hearts.

Twenty metres, fifteen metres! Was there no way of escape? no possible means of salvation? Hold! Gröning, the quiet thoughtful Gröning became our saviour!

He knelt beside me on the platform, with his rifle levelled, and sent shot after shot into the target which was now so close. Suddenly he thought of the way to save us.

'The helmsman!' he shouted out, and jumped up; 'everyone aim at the helmsman!'

The helmsman stood at the wheel of the *Ormea* in the usual mahogany wheel-house, with glass windows all round, and sought with set face for the spot where he would deliver us a deadly blow. We saw the man in his whole breadth quite distinctly standing there in front of us.

Gröning's idea, which was to be the means of saving us, was acted upon immediately. We stopped the senseless shooting at the dangerous bow, which had approached us as if by magic, and took our aim at the man who was guiding the enemy towards us. Hardly had the first salvo been fired, when there was a gurgling scream, the Englishman threw his arms up, fell forward on the wheel, slipped sideways to the deck, and clutching at the wheel-spokes, pulled the wheel round with him as he fell. The whole thing was like a miracle, which, even now, when I think of it, seems almost incredible. It was our salvation in desperate, most desperate circumstances.

The bow, which would have destroyed us, was only three metres away from its target when the rudder, which had been turned hard a-starboard, pulled it round, so that it stuck in the air, without touching us. The helmsman, who had been pierced by our bullets, and who fell on his wheel and turned it round, by so doing ruined in his death-fall the work of his hands, which had been so nearly successful.

To show how dangerously close the tug was when the wheel was thrown over, it may be mentioned that her stern in turning did not pass clear of us, but struck us a good hard blow and left behind as a remembrance a shallow bump on the diving tank.

As the wild beast after a false spring retreats like a coward and does not attempt a second, so also did our *Bull-dog* depart from us and seek safety in rapid flight under cover of heavy rolling smoke-clouds. The whistling of our bullets and the loss of his helmsman had apparently subdued the surly little tug captain. But it must be allowed that the rascal was plucky, and we all recognised that fully, when we had recovered from our tremendous fright and were trying to remember how everything had happened.

Silently I shook Gröning by the hand, and with a smile tapped that spot on his breast where a place is kept free for the reward of heroic acts of this nature by order of His Majesty the Kaiser. Today that spot on his breast is decorated with the silver and black of the Iron Cross.

What further shall I relate of the adventures which were yet to come on this journey, but which were so lacking in interest and danger after those we had already gone through and which I have described at length? The crisis of the voyage was passed when the *Ormea* affair lay behind us, and when the crisis has been reached, I think the remainder of the tale should be briefly told. To those whom it may interest I will disclose the fact that we did not permit the sailing ship to escape as she tried to do, but chased her and torpedoed her without further ado, when the crew had left her; that in the dusk of evening of the same day, we had the luck to take yet another valuable prize, as we sunk a steamer heavily laden with meat, which had come from Sydney; that we cruised about for several days more in our sphere of operations, the good times alternating with the bad; that Schweckerle had to bite the sour apple on several more occasions, as his children faithlessly forsook him one after the other. But he had this to comfort him, that none of his pupils denied their good education or forgot his careful attentions to their needs. They all ran straight and true and hit their target. There were many pleasant events to be noted down in our log book, and here and there some small excitements with which the destroyers and patrol boats of the enemy punctuated our day's work, so as to prevent us from getting swollen-headed and careless.

The day came when I decided to start on our homeward journey. We had expended nearly all our torpedoes and shells; oil, water, and provisions were so far reduced as to make our return journey appear precarious. We could not tell in advance what the weather was going to be like on our homeward journey, and whether or not we should be delayed by unforeseen and unsought for storm and contrary winds.

I decided not to go by the same route on our voyage homewards as we had followed on our way out. The Witches'

Cauldron with its horrors was still too fresh in our memory. Better far to make a detour now that we had successfully accomplished our task rather than harass ourselves with dangers which we could avoid. On the thirteenth day after setting out on our journey our nerves were not in such good condition or so capable of withstanding strain as to make us desirous of carrying out fresh experiments with them.

CHAPTER XVII

STORM

THUS it came about that on the fifteenth day of our voyage, when we encountered the great storm which gave us an anxious time for many days, we found ourselves far away up in the North Atlantic, there where the warm spring air crouches shuddering for a long time in its winter cloak, and where the sun never rises high, because it is not worth his while, as the icy nor'-west wind which blows up here for three-quarters of the year would destroy his warmth in any case.

For some time past we had got out reluctantly once more our thick camel's-hair things, which we had discarded disdainfully down there in the south. As we passed from parallel to parallel on our northerly course the coverings in which we wrapped ourselves increased.

And now to the considerable cold was added the storm – a storm of which I have never seen the like during my whole time of service, and to which I desire therefore to dedicate a few lines, because a storm in a U-boat is something quite special.

The behaviour of the barometer had appeared to me to be

not entirely satisfactory during the past two days. Its constant
rising and falling, coupled with winds which arose suddenly,
led me to expect bad weather. It was during the night of the
24th and 25th of April. We were running submerged at a great
depth during the night and I was lying half-undressed on my
bunk and asleep. Towards two o'clock in the morning I was
awakened by the stoker of the watch, who announced to me:
'Lieutenant Petersen begs the Captain to come into the control-
room. He can no longer control the boat.' I pulled on my jacket
and ran aft quickly. I noticed on the way the violent inclination
which the boat had got, and I knew from that what was happen-
ing up topsides. It must be a really big gale with a sea such as
only the powerful free Atlantic can produce, for anywhere else
it would be unthinkable that we should be subjected to so much
motion at a depth of twenty metres.

Petersen confirmed my opinion about the storm, which must
have arisen during the night, and strengthened his assertion by
stating that he had never encountered such difficulties with the
depth-rudders in all his experience on board. That meant a good
deal, as Petersen had been on board with me since the ship
commissioned and had already sampled all sorts of bad weather.
In spite of all the skill and attention lavished by him and the
well-trained *personnel*, the power of the depth-rudders was not
sufficient to overcome the tremendous force of the waves. The
boat was tossed upwards and chucked down again, as if absolutely rudderless. Only when we had doubled the depth at which
we had been travelling hitherto, was it at all possible for us to
steady the boat, and even then we could feel the heavy sea. It
must have been a terrific storm.

When we came to the surface, as soon as it was light in the
morning, it was absolutely out of the question to open the
hatchway. The sea had worked itself up into a foaming fury.
Masses of water as high as houses came rolling on, opal green
in colour, covered with long white foam-streaks and crowned
with a wreath of spray and raging white froth. Each of these
tossing, raging mountains hurled itself upon us and buried us
with a thunderous report in its bosom, flooding the decks and
even the high conning-tower to a depth of several metres. Any

one of us who had opened the hatch and ventured to go on top of the conning-tower would have been helplessly swept away by the next attack of the wild sea, and drowned.

I stood at the periscope and watched from there the raging of the elements. It seemed to me as if we were in a range of mountains, so high and tremendous appeared the walls of water which our boat had to scale, so deep and steep the declivities down which we plunged heavily, nose-first. To look far into the distance was out of the question. I could only see from one high crest to the next, which appeared even higher, and whatever was beyond that vanished in the clouds of spray which filled the air, and hid behind the shreds of foam which the storm tore loose and carried with it, and disappeared into the pearly grey clouds which passed over the water, howling and threatening. Masses of broken clouds brought rainstorms crashing down in their train and made the sky half as dark as night. It was difficult to believe that somewhere in that dark dirty heaven the sun must be shining. I could more easily believe that he had temporarily overslept himself and that the heavens were shrieking for him angrily. The boat was labouring hard and with extreme difficulty in the storm. The whole structure cracked and trembled when from the conning-tower on high a sea came plunging down into the depths and with thunderous roar buried the bow right under the trough of the wave. And under the constant bumps and buffets we suffered very considerably ourselves. We had to hold on to something constantly, to cling to any oily object, in order not to fall down. Everywhere one knocked and squashed oneself. Nowhere could rest or quiet be found, because no chair or object remained standing unless it was well and firmly secured. We became in the end quite tired and limp from the unceasing bodily motion in which the rolling of the boat kept us, and from the damp heavy air which squeezed through all the chinks and made all the cupboards swell, and from the loss of sleep and appetite, which resulted from all the other discomforts.

The storm raged for three days and three nights with undiminished fury. Then the skies became clearer, the wind decreased in strength, and the rolling sea became gradually calmer. At noon on the third day the sun broke through the clouds for the first time. Shortly before this we had ventured to open the hatch, and we greeted the first sunbeam, though we had to pay for the pleasure of seeing it with a cold-water bath.

CHAPTER XVIII

HOMEWARD BOUND

FOR three days we had been driven along by the storm, losing all sense of direction, so it was little wonder that we welcomed the good pilot, the sun, with a cheery greeting and quickly fetched our sextants in order to ascertain our position. Our calculations showed that we had remained practically stationary during the whole period, and had not got any nearer home. But what did that matter to us! The storm was dying away, the sea becoming smooth, and our good trusty boat had once more given proof of her worth, and had remained hale and hearty in spite of all the storms. We found ourselves in the North Sea in the afternoon of the next day, and with happy hearts altered course to the southward. Every metre, every mile, every hour brought us nearer home. Who that has not experienced it, can imagine the joy that fills the heart of a U-boat man when, after a long and successful voyage, he sees his home getting nearer! When he turns over the leaves of his war-diary and reads with astonishment those scribbled lines which tell of wonderful joys and terrible dangers, he holds his head and asks himself: 'You have lived through all that?'

Who can gauge the intense joy which passes through the breast of a U-boat captain when he sits down at his narrow writing-table and carefully writes out the account for his superior officers at home: 'Have destroyed X steamships, X sailing vessels!'

Everywhere in the whole boat are happy beaming faces. All worry and all danger have disappeared, and are forgotten with the buoyancy of youth and the flexibility of the nerves.

30th April, 9.30 a.m.

'Get out the lead' (now that it is calm we are travelling in the Bight – in the German Bight!).

'Exactly twenty-four metres,' announced boatswain's mate Lomann, who had remained on top of the conning-tower since four o'clock, from sheer joy at homecoming, in spite of the fact that he had been relieved of his watch at eight o'clock. He wanted to be the first to sight the land, as he was proud of his good eyesight, and was as pleased as a child if he managed to catch a glimpse of it a little sooner than his captain.

'Twenty-four metres – just see how that agrees with the chart,' I shouted to the helmsman, who was perched in the conning-tower with the chart upon his knees.

'Yes, absolutely right,' he called back, after he had compared the sounding with our calculated position.

'How far are we off the land?'

'Eight and a half miles!'

Five minutes later the low sand-banks of the German North Sea islands came into sight ahead of us. Now we could not do otherwise than tear our caps from our heads and wave them joyously round in circles, whilst our loud cheers greeted the sight of our native land. They passed down the conning-tower into the boat, and were repeated right fore and aft, and even succeeded in inflaming the heart of Schweckerle, who was seated forward between his empty torpedo-tubes, lonely and lacking a job of work.

A short time later we were travelling up the estuary of our home river. Proudly our distinguishing pendants fluttered on the mast, announcing to all the ships we met: 'Here comes U-202.' Our message told them all that we came from a far journey. Everywhere we passed we met with a respectful and enthusiastic reception. Officers and men crowded in thick masses on the upper decks of their ships, and right into our innermost hearts penetrated the cry from a hundred voices:

'Three cheers for Submarine U-202! Hurrah! hurrah! hurrah!'

Thus was a small drenched U-boat received by the proud German fleet.

At three o'clock in the afternoon of the 30th April we made fast in the U-boat harbour.

Another title in the **MEWS** series

F.A.T.E. 1:
Galaxy of the Lost

by Gregory Kern

Captain Kennedy, Earth's trouble shooter, carries the Banner of Terran against the unknown sciences and alien psychologies of a thousand worlds.

The crack in the cosmos that has to be sealed!

F.A.T.E. is the space hero series that has become a must wherever Science Fiction is read. A solid space adventure more exciting than 'Startrek' and far more real than 'Perry Rhodan'.

On sale at newsagents and booksellers everywhere.

Another title in the **MEWS** series

Spider 1:
Death Reign of the
Vampire King

by Grant Stockbridge

The Spider – all his resources are required against
this hideous new menace. For battalions of trained
vampire bats, starved so that they would attack any
living thing, their teeth annointed with deadly poison,
are being set loose in dozens of cities. Thousands
have succumbed to their lethal kisses. No one knows
where they will strike next . . .

Only The Spider could discover their hideout and
stop the man who controlled them and was bent
upon total domination of mankind. But would he be
in time before the deadly kisses of the vampire
legion brought a whole nation to its knees?

On sale at newsagents and booksellers everywhere.

MEWS BESTSELLERS

NEL P.O. BOX 11, FALMOUTH TR10 9EN, CORNWALL.

For U.K.: Customers should include to cover postage, 19p for the first book plus 9p per copy for each additional book ordered up to a maximum charge of 73p.

For B.F.P.O. and Eire: Customers should include to cover postage, 19p for the first book plus 9p per copy for the next 6 and thereafter 3p per book.

For Overseas: Customers should include to cover postage, 20p for the first book plus 10p per copy for each additional book.

Name ....

Address...

....

....

Title ....

Whilst every effort is made to maintain prices, new editions or printings may carry an increased price and the actual price of the edition supplied will apply.